The Soul's Journey III:
A Case Study

Tom Jacobs

By Tom Jacobs

Books

The Soul's Journey I: Astrology, Reincarnation, and Karma with a Medium and Channel
The Soul's Journey II: Emotional Archaeology
Chiron, 2012, and the Aquarian Age: The Key and How to Use It
Lilith: Healing the Wild
Saturn Returns: Thinking Astrologically
Living Myth: Exploring Archetypal Journeys
Seeing Through Spiritual Eyes: A Memoir of Intuitive Awakening

E-book

Pluto's 2012 Retrograde and the First Square to Uranus in Aries

Channeled Material

Approaching Love
Understanding Loss and Death
Goddess Past, Present, and Future
Conscious Revolution: Tools for 2012 and Beyond
Djehuty Speaks (a collection of the four books above)

Natal Reports

The True Black Moon Lilith Natal Report
Living in the Present Tense Natal Report

Fiction

The Book of John Corbett
Kyle: Theme and Variations
Modern Love: Erotic Vignettes, Vol. 1

ISBN-13: 978-1484068588
ISBN-10: 1484068580

Acknowledgements

A number of people come and gone over the last decade have triggered me to become aware of the stories contained in this book. Some of them also held space for me to work through them! I would like to thank family, friends, and lovers for sharing their time and energy with me as this process has unfolded.

I've worked with some talented, heart-centered professionals to get to the bottom of life issues and the other-life stories behind them. My thanks go to them for their insights and support.

I would like to thank Jillian Sheridan for her support as I live these stories and put them all down on paper. The writing process has involved direct remembering of some difficult aspects of my other-life stories and her support has been invaluable.

Opening

This 3rd installment of The Soul's Journey story expands upon the previous two as it shifts focus and gets specific. *The Soul's Journey I: Astrology, Reincarnation, and Karma with a Medium and Channel* introduces the concepts central to my evolutionary astrology work that are informed and shaped by channeling and mediumship. It presents a 4-step method of chart analysis, the skeleton of which I learned from Steven Forrest in his Apprenticeship Program meetings. I then edited and updated it after several years of tutoring by and channeling an Ascended Master about the nature of soul and its multilife journey and working as a psychic medium with the spirits of the dead. *The Soul's Journey II: Emotional Archaeology* takes 7 people's lives and karmic histories as examples while I teach them the process that I call emotional archaeology. That process is one of digging down through the strata of an individual's emotional history in order to catalogue his or her emotions and learn to work with them in conscious ways. This includes understanding karma and changing the deep beliefs that comprise it.

I am happy with those first two books and eager to tell you the rest of the story. This 3rd volume in the series takes a different approach by focusing on one individual's journey of self-discovery and integration of what we have been taught to call past lives. Here these will be referred to as the soul's other lives. I am the case study about which you will read in these pages. I want to make it clear now that this is not because I can't keep my own counsel or because I don't get enough attention at home. It is because I am motivated to use one person's stories to describe the larger and longer karmic journey set out by his or her soul in terms of life experiences and their correlates to other spots on the Earth timeline and I have been working with my own emotions and other-life, karmic stories in one way or another for almost a decade. Presenting to you the appropriate scope and breadth of information about a person who is not me would require quite a long time to collect information through counseling sessions with another individual, even though my client files are rich with other-life stories I help my clients to integrate and heal. Part of that appropriate scope and breadth involves presenting numerous examples of multiple chart configurations so that the variety of experiences over the course of many lives is adequately fleshed out. A single chart configuration can point to a myriad of multilife experiences as a soul learns about the right way to handle work, relationships, learning, family, sex, and anything else. It is important to me at this stage to flesh this out for you using one person's life story and the example of this Tom Jacobs person is readily at hand.

I am sensitive about sharing so much personal information and in fact feel rather vulnerable doing it. The opportunity to explain all of this in a way that tells the complete story inspires me, so here we are. In my mind transforming our view of ourselves and life itself is the next step in the evolution of the species and this book is intended to give you a glimpse into my own transformative process.

A New Framework to View Human Lives: Manifestations of Soul

Past Lives Are Other Lives

The notion of past lives is ready to be tossed out because we are in fact multidimensional beings existing all along the Earth timeline. *The consciousness of each individual exists outside time.* We are timeless beings having temporary human experiences and our language regarding our human lives should reflect this.

Saying that we are energetic beings is a form of saying that we are portions of consciousness. In many places when I write and teach about this I realize I am influenced by the perspective of Ascended Master Djehuty (a.k.a. Thoth, St. Germain, and Merlin), the primary being I channel. He describes what we are in different terms: portions of All That Is, Divine Consciousness or Intelligence, Source, Goddess, God, and Universe among others. His intention is to help us see the bigger picture of soul and consciousness and how each of us is incarnating in the time-space dimension and living numerous lives on Earth spread out all along its timeline in order to learn about what it means to do so. The requirements, costs, effects, and results of making choices while embodied is the name of the game here on Earth for us energetic beings and ultimately – according to Djehuty – we will each learn the truth about our most important mission here: what love is, where it comes from, and who is responsible for giving it to whom. Over time we'll find ourselves on all possible sides of the entire variety of available human interactions in order for our souls to explore life and each other. Each human life of each of us is an opportunity to do so.

In many given lives we tend to identify with our human minds and bodies and we let those minds decide what our experiences mean. Over time we in this way develop karma, which is made up of beliefs about why things happen (and don't happen). These beliefs create knots and bubbles in our energy fields that in turn vibrate more of the same into our lives. It is true that our beliefs create our realities and lives. When we work with karma as a set of beliefs about why things do and don't happen then it is easy to see that karma can in fact be changed.[1]

The impetus to write this book is a desire to explain the process of identifying karma and changing it. I have done this through a series of experiences that have put me in direct touch with portions of consciousness of other manifestations of my soul. We have been taught to call these portions of consciousness past lives but it no longer seems accurate or appropriate do so given the view of soul,

---

[1] See *The Soul's Journey I* and *The Soul's Journey II* for detailed information on this topic.

life, and the nature of humans to which I've been exposed. My training, tutoring, and expansion of consciousness under the watchful eye of Ascended Master Djehuty has enlarged and transformed the lens through which I see and experience all aspects of life. Instead of as past lives Djehuty invites us to see that these life stories on other parts of the timeline that are not you but are associated with your soul. They are in certain ways parallel to your own individual life story as the mission of soul is repeated in each life. He lays out a vision of soul as a portion of consciousness that is simultaneously extended into many discrete individuals spread out along the entirety of the Earth timeline. We have been trained to view history as linear and to view ourselves as a result of and tied to time because our bodies are tied to time – there is a time when our bodies do not exist and then we are born, mature, and die. This lends itself to seeing ourselves as the products of the times in which we live in ways that do not allow for the complexity and multidimensionality of what is really going on with us as energetic beings, as soul extended into human form temporarily. Djehuty asks us to explore a different vision: *We are energetic beings with consciousness that exist outside time temporarily embodied to learn about certain processes possible only while embodied.*

That there are many of these life stories along the Earth timeline does not mean that any or each one of them is not incredibly important. A life that lasts a few days or years is just as important as one that lasts 100 years or more. The same is true regarding lives in which nothing or a lot seems to happen. A life in which nothing of apparent import unfolds (yes, we each have lived a large number of boring lives!) is just as important as one in which we participate in grand social movements or in some other way contributes something essential to our community or human or social evolution. Each of these lives is important because the social, filial, cultural, political, religious, educational, economic, and other conditions in play at various points along the Earth timeline present unique parameters and incubators for the human to explore the karmic journey the soul has set out for its many human manifestations.

As an example let's say that a major learning the soul sets out to learn over a number of different lives is empowerment through education (Pluto in the 3rd house). In some lives the humans associated with that soul will have seemingly unlimited access to and, therefore, empowerment through education. In other lives other humans associated with this same soul will experience full-on blocks to and lacks of educational resources and, as a result, an absence or dearth of empowerment through education (experienced as powerlessness or feeling overpowered). The humans experiencing different sides of this life learning theme will be dealing with their emotions and thoughts that arise from the scenarios. These thoughts and feelings can create beliefs that become solidified and knee-jerk positioned in the person's energy field to the point of becoming karma, which is stored in the energy field as knots and bubbles. From the soul's perspective however the highs and lows are equal. The soul does not get stressed when its human manifestations – you and me and everyone else – feel disempowered, small, irrelevant, or weak. The soul also does not rejoice when you and I achieve something we've been working toward or feel celebrated for who we are or what we do. The soul – always outside time – learns that given a particular mix of social, filial, cultural, and other factors, certain choices yield certain kinds of results and that those results inspire the human to form and attach to certain kinds of beliefs about the genesis and existence of those results. This is what it comes to Earth in embodied form to learn – what it is like to be here making choices and dealing with the effects of those choices.

Here is the big picture unfolding behind the scenes: The soul is sitting outside space-time (the dimension in which Earth and life upon it exists) watching you and your cohorts across the Earth timeline (what we have been trained to call past lives) make choices and deal with the consequences. It is checking your various experiences off from a list of possible experiences available to a human as it watches you go through your decision-making, life, emotional, and all other processes during life. In one life you get a chest infection and don't do anything about it. You spit up blood and decide it's nothing and in time you die from it. The soul checks that experience off the list – "death resulting from not listening to the loud and clear signals of the body" – and moves on to watch other yous situated along different parts of the timeline in how they might respond to such a situation. In some other life you might get a similar infection, cough up blood, and go to a health care professional right away. In this life you feel good about taking proactive measures for your health, living to see another day because you listened to the loud and clear signals of your body. In this case the soul checks this off the list and, again, moves on.

All experiences we have and choices we make in response suit and support the learning journey of the soul. *It is important to understand that the soul does not judge, fear, regret, or shame any of our choices. We cannot offend or injure the soul.* This is because it is a portion of consciousness existing outside space-time and not affected by the damage we do to our human selves or experience. Soul never forgets its nature as an energetic being – or as Djehuty would say, a Divine being – and each human is an extension of soul into embodied reality. We could be thought of as players acting out the intentions of soul while we have forgotten that soul is behind it all while the entire time soul forgets nothing.

It is also important to understand that soul is not in charge of our lives. Soul does not conform to the vision of judging, controlling god that we may have somehow let stick in our minds. Soul is not pulling the strings of our lives. We cannot appeal to soul to help us dig ourselves out of difficulty but consulting the wisdom of soul can definitely help us correct beliefs, choices, and behaviors that we use to steer ourselves wrong or into painful dynamics. Our free will is everything and exercising it is on one level the entire point that we bother to incarnate here as we do. Soul is in fact passively observing our reactions to and choices regarding the life learning themes that it has set out for us.

As we are energetic beings, our level of vibration is everything. Thoughts, emotions, ideas, and beliefs vibrate the world around each person into existence. Why does one person learning about free will as a life learning theme feel constricted while another feels entirely free? Why does one person learning about family connections as a theme feel disconnected from all he or she came from while another feels accepted and safe within his or her family? The beliefs, emotions, thoughts, and ideas we develop through experiences vibrate opportunities and dynamics (and the lack of them) into our spheres.

We can know something is true of us and yet not find it that part of us welcome in our worlds. The reflection from those around us can seem to indicate that something critical about us isn't true or, at minimum, might not be welcome. A belief could be behind this and changing the belief would change the vibration emitted by a person. The altered vibration would then draw or magnetize new kinds of situations, relationships, and opportunities to a person and these could be acted upon in order to change how life unfolds.

Believing and living as though our essence is tied to time, we can get into the habit of thinking of the other lives of our souls as past lives. When we do this we frame ourselves in a way that asserts that we are products of our histories. From the human perspective this is true but the work I offer intends to expose you to a different perspective in which your essence is defined as consciousness and exists across time. If we think of ourselves as the products of history then it follows that we are the way we are because of what has happened to us and what we have chosen to do.

The importance of moving away from thinking of our other selves along the Earth timeline as past lives – as past selves – cannot be overemphasized. Looking at these other lives associated with your soul across the timeline is neither invitation nor license to view some perceived defect of personality or apparent weakness in the self as the product of a past that cannot be changed. This work, in other words, should not be used to excuse present behaviors in light of something that happened to the self in another life. We are all responsible for ourselves in the present moment – what we choose to do, how we choose to react to situations in our lives, the meaning we ascribe to what happens, and what we choose to do in response are up to us at all times.

As you will explore in these pages, I have done what I can to take information gained from exploration of my soul's other lives through various means to serve the process of becoming more present in my life. I do not use it justify feelings, states of consciousness, choices, or perceptions of brokenness and shortcomings but instead work toward cleaning up the present by using this information reclaimed from other parts of the timeline. I have made the decision to be in conscious, aware, responsible charge of my life now and I challenge you to do the same.

Changing Karma and the Idea of What a Human Is

Changing beliefs can change karma. This is an easy enough concept to work with when you can have a bit of faith in it. It is true that some of our beliefs and karmas run deep and working with this concept can be challenging. Sometimes special techniques need to be employed to strengthen our faith in our right to believe something different than a limiting belief we've carried for a long time that we think is or must be who we are. We form identities attached to our beliefs and this is one reason why some prove difficult to change. Most of us are not aware of our beliefs and so do not receive training to discern the helpful ones from those that are limiting and don't serve us. *When faced with shedding an identity formed as a result or extension of a belief we are tasked with letting go of a piece of who we may think we are.* What is waiting for us is a more direct experience of ourselves as conscious beings creating life around us but we like our ideas of who we are.

This process therefore invites – but, really, requires – that we upgrade our vision of who and what and who we are. This is where the perspective that we are energetic beings temporarily having human experiences begins to be handy. When we adapt to this view of who we are and learn the ins and outs of working with ourselves as such we find it much easier to deal with strong beliefs because we have tools to work in compassionate, healing ways with the parts of us that carry difficult emotions and identities attached to the deeply-held beliefs. If we believe we are our ideas then we get attached to them. If we believe that our emotions are who we are then we have no chance of constructively working with them, releasing the past, and getting present to the experience of ourselves as energetic beings, what I've been shown and believe strongly is our next evolutionary step as a species.

As an example of identity formed with and attached to a belief, take someone who believes that her voice is not going to be heard. There will be some important, formative experiences in at least a handful of that soul's human lives along the Earth timeline in which it is true that she is not heard. Each time it is difficult and painful for those humans related to her soul to find this out; there is emotional pain accompanying the realization. Perhaps at one spot on the timeline she was told in a scathing way by a loved one that her opinion doesn't matter and no one wants to hear from her. The sting would inspire her mind to develop a strategy to use going forward to prevent that pain from occurring again in other situations. This is one of the amazing talents a human mind develops: it is always on guard, watching and waiting for the repeat in the present moment of scenarios and circumstances from the past that lead to pain. The work of the mind in this case would end up with a reason that the painful situation occurred and her actions, the actions of others, circumstances, or all of this will be used by her mind to explain why the situation unfolded as it did and why the pain was encountered. Later in life – and also bleeding through to other lives – she will find herself in situations that ring the bell of the emotional memory of the past event. It will seem to portend a repeat of the past painful experience and she will act in a way prescribed by her mind that is intended to avoid being hurt again. It could be that she doesn't speak at all, withholding her opinion. Or it could be that she gingerly tests the waters of the personalities around her in order to ascertain how much space she is allowed to take up in the given circumstances, often based on her perceptions of the others involved. Alternatively it could be that she chooses to dive in head-long and say what's on her mind even if others don't want to hear it and may react negatively. No matter where she falls in the range of possibilities she will confront a belief within herself about why past pain happened and/or why her voice will or will not be heard in the given situation.

To be fair, she does not have to reinforce the belief offered up by her mind. But most humans think we are our minds and as a result tend to believe whatever our minds tell us is happening, is real, or could be happening or real. At each opportunity to share her opinion she can decide that hers matter and that she has the right to be heard. Each and every time in fact she can make a new decision that challenges, overrides, or overwrites the belief that has been in play. We each have this opportunity at every turn in our day-to-day lives: the chance to shed old models of who we are or should be that are based in our histories. We need to acknowledge that we are energetic beings shaped by our histories in emotional ways – humans experience energy and respond emotionally. And we need to see that we are as musical instruments designed to respond vibrationally to energetic stimulus in the world around us. We need to do all of this while learning to detach from our histories as the sum of who we are.

All human decisions are informed by beliefs but some of them are deeper than others. And it is true that all beliefs do not become karma. Some come into our fields and hang our for a bit and then leave, never getting solidified through reactions to repeated experience and therefore never becoming stuck in our energetic/emotional fields. Some come in and we try them on for size but find that they don't suit us. We might come from a family whose members carry some bigoted attitudes and spend some time trying to fit in, ultimately feeling out of place because we can't make those beliefs work for us. We could also be born into a family full of people with "make love, not war" as an energetic signature but have a deep karmic impulse to explore making war, unable to make those beliefs carried by our families work for us.

Other-Life Stories and How to Identify Them

The examples included here are all from my life or, better put, each reflects my increasing awareness of lives associated with my soul on other parts of the Earth timeline and my efforts to integrate them with my conscious personality now. There are some messed up beliefs among this cohort and I've done my best to work with them as bleed-throughs into my life now. I consider them in this way to prevent their fears, desires, and emotions from shaping my life in directions that don't work well for me. These portions of consciousness exist in other lives as their own separate beings with free will but in this life, the one in which I am named Tom Jacobs and am stirring up and spilling words every which way, my free will is what matters most. I am supposed to be the point person in this menagerie; I am the one who needs to be making the decisions. It behooves me to recognize all of these parts while maintaining a grounded sense of being in charge of my life. As you will read in these pages this can be challenging at times but I have learned how to come back to myself and stay in charge of my life while carrying the knowledge and wisdom of other parts with me as I go while never letting them take over once I meet and learn about how to work with them.

There is no exact number of human lives we live on Earth and we each live a high number of incredibly boring lives. These are those in which we do what we seem to be expected to do, getting up at the same time every day and doing regular things like punching a clock. I joke about how many people might prefer to remember being Napoleon because it is so prevalent for us to want to have been someone important that we'll even settle for having been a super intense megalomaniac bent on ego gratification. But the fact remains that the point of being on Earth is not in being well-known for something but in making choices and dealing with the consequences of those choices – expressing free will and creating a life as a result.

In any of our lives we won't remember most of our other lives. What you will read about here references fewer than two dozen lives associated with my soul that number perhaps in the many thousands or more. What we remember are the feelings related to situations and dynamics in some lives that have stuck with us as more painful or more joyful than others. We carry many emotions related to other lives – those that bleed through and inform and affect us today – but it's true that there are categories of those feelings that persist in many lives. One example would be the woman's pain in the example above from not being heard. For the humans associated with that soul the theme and related experiences will persist in many of their Earth-bound lives and yet not all will stand out enough to bleed through and be re-experienced in other lives associated with that soul. The most painful and those to which the most and deepest meaning have been attached are the ones that are potential candidates for bleeding through into her life today.

I do remember scenes from some lives of social, religious, and political influence. With my Pluto in the

12th house in some lives my human selves think big. Sometimes it's thinking universally as in spiritually and mystically and at other times it is to do with the masses of people that make up humanity, working to have an effect on a large scale. Both are equally prevalent and valid 12th-house themes for someone with Pluto there to explore over the course of many lives. I also remember being tied to a door as a slave and seeing absolutely nothing fulfilling about being alive. We all have a range of experiences over the course of many lives on Earth.

My South Node of the Moon is in the 10th house and this means that a route that my soul chooses for my human selves to be conditioned through involves learning about the ups and downs of creating a public persona, dealing with the consequences of living life in public, and being a symbol for others of the work I do in the world. Anyone who lives in the 10th house will tell you that there are nice things about being well-known (scale is always relative) and some not-so-nice things (everyone sees you and no one knows who you are is one but there are others). But these lives of relative fame and privilege are no more important to the soul and from the soul's perspective than lives of slavery or something similar or amazingly normal lives filled to the brim with boring day-to-day routine. It's all the same – it all teaches the soul about what it incarnates to learn about being human and the life learning themes chosen by the soul.[2]

A Milestone in Expanding Consciousness

This project is in fact a milestone in a long healing process of making peace with the past and coming to be present. It is the best way I can think of to appropriately organize and understand a number of the other-life files I've collected and have been making notes on for almost a decade. I considered writing something along these lines

---

[2] One reason I was initially hesitant to share these stories or write a book like this is that we should be skeptical when hearing someone say that he or she is the reincarnation of some well-known figure. With my South Node in the 10th house and the exploits related to that in various lives there are some lives in which my soul's manifestations are somewhat well-known (scale is always relative), including one included in this list anonymously. But there are many more lives in which manifestations of my soul just wish someone knew them as more than property to be used and abused, in which those mes crave something interesting to do that can have an effect on the world on any scale. Regarding soul journeys that involve the 10th house it begs mentioning that infamy and public hatred are at times par for the course – the other side of the "being well known in public" trip. None of the material in this book is intended to stroke my ego in any way or, conversely, paint me as a victim to anything or anyone (other than to myself through certain bone-headed choices that are part and parcel of all learning journeys).

several times over the past few years but always hesitated and put it off due to a worry that it might be or seem self-indulgent or somehow self-aggrandizing, even if I only were to write only about incredibly boring lives. Far from it, in fact. You're going to be reading a number of things about which I tend to be embarrassed and I only rarely share with anyone if at all. Sometimes clients have heard bits of a few of these stories to underscore a point I'm making about the various ways that life learning themes are expressed and experienced in different lives or the importance of understanding, compassion, or forgiveness, but I have certainly not broadcast most of this information widely. I am interested in sharing these stories and in you receiving them in the spirit of increasing and deepening self-understanding and self-acceptance so that we all can get a bit more present to who we really are as energetic beings.

This piece of writing in front of you reflects personal stories that are close to my heart for a number of reasons. This is primarily because in uncovering these stories and fragments of stories over the years I have come to understand who I am on deeper levels than I otherwise would have. Knowing that I am a male human named Tom Jacobs born in Dover, Ohio, USA, Earth in the year of someone's lord 1972 is a level of detail useful for some applications yet doesn't tell me who I am. My passions regarding art, music, literature, comedy, and theater are real but do not answer any "whys" about me that I have always carried. My fear of the liminal space between

27

waking and sleep in a core way defines my experience of me but looking at and feeling it doesn't explain anything about me to myself. Discovering these life threads relayed here – facets and experiences of these other personalities who are active on the Earth timeline living their own lives and in a mostly-subdued way bleeding through into my life now – explains me to me. For almost a decade now I've been building a collage of these pieces of memories from other lives (other people's lives!) that define me and I feel it's fair to say that this process has been a beginning in my experience of being okay with being alive and, even, being happy about it. Seeds of peace have been sown within me by putting words and images to the feelings I've carried my whole life about who I am that goes beyond my biographical data and experience in this single life as Tom Jacobs.

You'll read 19 life stories below that I consider bleed-throughs from other lives associated with my soul. You might notice that all but one are male. There is no reason for this I can offer other than as a man in this life as Tom Jacobs I am encountering certain issues that I suppose could be said to fit better with the experience of being a man but I do not know for sure. We each live more or less equal numbers of male and female lives as humans in order to learn all possible ways of exploring a wide variety of life learning themes. That I've remembered mostly male lives probably doesn't mean that I've lived more lives as a man than as a woman. It might be a safe bet to say that my life themes this time around tie in with being a man and so this is the majority of what has been recalled.

The stories are organized more or less chronologically according to when I became aware of them, not necessarily when I resolved the issues. Some of them unfold slowly over a period of months or years (the durations of my piecing together details to understand a story fully) and they are laid out here in as best a timeline as is possible. Some are longer than others and some don't provide much in the way of detail. But the fact is that such portions of self are available to anyone primarily through feeling and not always through imagery, thought, and word-based memory. In my experience when these latter elements are known it is the result of following an emotion rising to or on the surface and letting the blanks be filled in by giving the part of self a voice – it always begins for me with an emotion. A key in my experience to working with these portions of soul and self from other lives is to isolate and identify a feeling and then put words to it, allowing sometimes an image or wisp of emotion to become fleshed out. In my case (and when doing this with and for clients) I'm grounded to the Earth enough to sense when something that is not me in this present moment rises to the surface.[3] Then I engage in a process of enquiry that asks questions of the energy or part of self to see what

---

[3] I imagine sending energetic cords from the bottoms of my feet and my root or 1st chakra to open my body up to draw the calming, grounding energy of the Earth into my body. I let my frequency be altered through this process.

sticks. I ask a question and see if it resonates "yes" or "no." In many people this can be experienced by learning to observe the flow of their energy fields and bodies. They might feel their heart, throat, or belly or other part of the body feel open or constricted in response to a stimulus. Open means "yes" or "true" (or "closer to yes" or "truer") and constricted indicates the opposite.

It is possible that my process is unique to me. Anyone who has learned to trust his or her intuition, inner wisdom, and/or guidance will have a unique process of discerning what is true for him or her. I hope that in these examples you are able to see how I in each case became aware of a feeling and then followed it within myself, allowing in time words and images to come to the surface to tell me the story so that I could do something productive with healing an imbalance in emotion, thought, or belief from other lives.

I don't expect that my process will make sense to everyone but I do intend that you learn at least something valuable about understanding the multilife journey of soul from what follows.

Isn't This Life Enough?

I've been asked in classes and lectures in joking and exasperated tones, "Isn't this life enough?" It's a fair question given how we've been conditioned to conceive of ourselves and our lives as humans. The answer is yes or no but depends entirely upon what kind of human reality you are interested in or willing to live in. Is a human a mind with a body or a body with a mind? Is a human the emotions he or she has? Is a human the sum of his or her experiences, accomplishments, and/or relationships? If your answer is yes to any of these questions then it is likely you will think this life is enough.

As it turns out, each life you live is an energetic and emotional composite of many lives. Certain emotions come to the surface in particular lives more than others but the emotional signatures from experiences that fit all the major life learning themes a soul signs up for are present in each of its human manifestations. *In other words you are a unique mosaic of the emotional imprints and contours that all yous across the timeline experience.*

If we think we are our emotions then those rooted in other parts of the Earth timeline can come up and recede without us thinking much of them. If they are who we are or part of who we are then their presence in our day-to-day lives doesn't stand out. Yet there are emotional reactions including fears that we have at certain times that are obviously out of proportion with the situation we are in or are dealing with in that moment. As I've experienced this I've learned a process to sense into and in time interview that corner of my consciousness (as you will read about in the rest of this volume) and found that more is going on than my linear, logical mind would tend to believe. As one example I have an intense fear of heights but there is no reason rooted in this life as Tom Jacobs. The first time I walked across the Golden Gate Bridge in

San Francisco I was transported in an intensely fearful place and feared I would fall or jump off it. The tension between the fear of an accident and the fear that I might choose to leap off the bridge brought an internal storm that made me nervous about all possibilities. I was with friends and was able to ground but it was frightening nonetheless. It was confusing and there is no issue in my life as Tom Jacobs to which I can point that can explain or justify those fearful reactions.

Today a friend told me about anger she was feeling. Her boyfriend had met a woman he found attractive and decided to be friends with her with no intention of pursuing anything further. She told me she was experiencing a rage toward someone for the first time. It was triggered by her boyfriend and wanted to head off in his direction even as she knew it wasn't about him. She wasn't interested in throwing the anger at him and was trying to figure it out. She recognized that in some other life she might have done something drastic when faced with the prospect of another woman coming into the picture or drawing her lover away from her. I asked her to own that she's angry and to let it be okay, to refrain from judging the ugly emotion and to do nothing from that place. She was "in it" as we spoke and several times said clearly and with certainty that she didn't like how it felt. The feeling filled her and she was getting to know a regular, normal, understandable human emotion that somehow had been left out in this life to that point.

This is what happens when an emotional imprint from another life surfaces. The best strategy I've come up with is to be with the feeling while staying grounded and in the body. Managing life as an emotional being isn't – as we seem to be taught – about stuffing ugly feelings down as much as we can, exploding later because we can't contain them, and blaming ourselves for being immature jerks. We're not doing life right if we only focus on the happy, kind, generous parts of us and deny the rest. Wholeness is impossible if we decide we are incapable of dealing with or uninterested in feeling distasteful feelings. Managing life as an emotional being isn't done well by avoiding feelings that we have and hiding them only to find distorted and twisted expressions later that seem outside of our control, which is what happens when something natural – something within us that seeks expression – is denied enough. *Operating ourselves consciously as energetic beings means allowing emotions of all kinds while consciously and responsibly dealing with them from a grounded state.*

My friend asked me today when you know that what you're experiencing is from this life – when are you just being you. I told her that we are each composites of human emotion and that things become triggered and rise to the surface when they do as invitations to integrate them. They are up – and in our faces – when it's time for that knot to unravel. Once we are able to cease judging those very normal human elements within us then we can keep perspective on all of our human experiences and understand our multidimensional nature.

In this book you will read 19 stories from my karmic history that I have needed to come to terms with and integrate in order to unravel a block or step into a new way of being in one part of life or another. There are more of which I'm aware that I'm choosing not to include. Some are left out because they are rather brief and the opportunity to learn from them seems overshadowed by others I've decided to include. Regarding others I'm simply not willing to relive those feelings at this moment in time. I live with the themes and am working with them on an ongoing basis but it seems important to have some intentions and boundaries since this project is about digging up and integrating difficult emotions and personas. I've decided that being gentle on myself is more important than spilling all the possible beans I could spill. Also it seems important to comment that I'm sure there will be more that come through and to the surface as time goes by. The publication of this book is by no means the end of the story. I feel I'm at a solid juncture point from which I can articulate clearly what I've learned thus far and am in the process of learning. As I continue down the path of my life there will be various challenges and invitations and a variety of emotions and feelings that go with them. I fully expect that as long as I'm alive I'll be feeling and feeling into what might be happening behind the scenes including on other points of the Earth timeline. Now that I know what is happening and how to do it, I'm actually looking forward to it!

A New Definition of Human

So, then, just what is a human? My definition in terms of the message of this book is this:

> *A human is a multidimensional energetic being temporarily living in a body. A human is capable of experiencing a wide variety of energetic stimulation that is felt as emotion. Given its multidimensional nature, a human has access to a broad spectrum of emotions across time connected to a wide variety of human lives associated sharing the same soul.*

The life you are presently living is enough if you want to consider that your experiences, choices, emotions, memories, desires, passions, fears, and dilemmas are who you are. This life is enough if you want it to be enough. But if we consider that we are our experiences, emotions, and histories from this life then we set ourselves up to miss entirely the bird's-eye view of ourselves as multidimensional beings and all that implies and offers – we miss the view on us that soul takes. For instance if I am how my parents treated me, the person who got that award, the person who failed a loved one, or the person who reneged on a promise, I eliminate the possibility that I can see the bigger picture of my life as an opportunity for soul to learn through my choices and their consequences.

Do you want to believe that you are the sum of your accomplishments? It's seductive, I admit. But if you do that then you set yourself up to also believe that you must be the sum of your failures. That never feels good to any of us unless we're into hating ourselves and keeping ourselves down. *I offer you that this life is a microcosm of a complex, multidimensional journey that spans millions of years across the Earth timeline. You are in essence a unique and necessary node on a network of conscious exploration of what life is like, means, calls for, requires, and costs when lived as a human having more or less forgotten your nature as an energetic being, as a Divine being.*

It is perfectly fine if you are not open to these perspectives at this time. If you have found this book then you are ready for one reason or another to encounter the perspectives, arguments, and stories it contains. You are of course free to choose how you view yourself and the notion of reincarnation. What I offer you in the rest of this material is an account of my experiences to gain awareness of soul as defined above and my place in its multidimensional, multilife journey as this dude named Tom Jacobs born in Dover, Ohio, Earth in November of 1972.

As I have lived through those experiences a new sense of identity has emerged. Imagine being in a noisy place with your eyes closed. At first what surrounds you will seem one mass of noise. Then you might notice a human voice, a machine noise, or foot steps that stand out. In truth each of the noises that combine to create a wall of sound has its own rhythm and contours. Living the processes outlined in this book has been akin to getting to know all the sounds in a noisy place one by one without opening my eyes. But the sound is emotion and belief and the noisy environment is my consciousness.

Anyone engaging in their own version of this process will find that at first the feelings can't always be discerned from each other. When we get into our hearts we might find a wall of emotion analogous to the wall of sound in a busy, noisy place in which all the sounds contribute to a mish-mash of auditory signals. Within each of us – even those of us fully and completely sure of our sanity – this is how consciousness is until we learn to work with awareness with what is in there. You already know that you have many different kinds of feelings and that at times one or a couple overshadow all the others and then fade to the background once again. In these pages what I am inviting you to do that is new is to explore your consciousness – your inner world and sense of self – to begin learning to discern the many emotions and emotional threads and patterns that are there. Each emotion correlates to an energetic state and a number of the emotions that you feel can at some point (when the timing is right) be traced and connected to situations and the accompanying karmas (beliefs) of manifestations of your soul living lives on other sections along the Earth timeline.

Sorting Through the Noise

Picking up on any particular other life is like picking noises out of a din. With sounds you listen with your ears and attempt to catch what presents its own rhythm. With emotions you keep your heart open and attentive and you do exactly the same thing. This requires being willing to feel all that is in your heart while being willing to release what does not belong to you – you have to clear your space of the unnecessary influences of energies and emotions you might have picked up from others or the places in which you've found yourself.

You might have an emotion that you recognize and consider is part of who you are. Over time you notice that it is triggered and brought to the surface by particular sorts of dynamics in your life. If you are willing to give it a voice and not simply stuff it down or react to it – hint, hint: these are important tools! – then you will in time be able to get to the know the part of you carrying the feeling being triggered. *If you do this enough you will begin to feel that it is not you who is speaking.* My experience of this has opened my eyes to consider a new definition of being human. This is so because if I don't discern the many parts of self represented by these different emotions then I believe that they are all me, or perhaps we could say that I will then believe they are who I am.

38

Learning the process described here and putting it into play wasn't exactly intentional. It was the outgrowth of tools learned from my early studies in what I today like to call *adventures in consciousness* and influences along the way such as the work of Buddhist meditation teacher Cheri Huber. The process of putting words to a feeling took some dedicated learning because the human tendency – and I am no different than anyone else in this regard – is to let a feeling take over and go with it, letting it drive us off an intended path and into the brush and/or a ditch because that part of us doesn't want us to get where we set out to go. Putting words to a voice for me involves feeling the emotion, refraining from any judgment of its existence or particular contours of expression (it might be mean, petty, silly, immature, etc.) and letting it rise to the surface periodically or regularly are keys to making this work. The part within you must know that you are willing to let it speak and you must be grounded enough to be willing to give air time to something within you that might have nothing nice to say about you, others, life, or all of creation. In time I learned to treat all parts of me that rise to the surface carrying a distasteful or embarrassing emotion as a friend I know and respect who is having a bad day and just needs to get something off his or her chest. I have friends who preface a bit of complaining or whining with a note that what is about to come out probably sounds or is silly, petty, immature, etc., and I do it, too. It's a useful exercise with friends because sometimes we need to hear ourselves saying the thing to another in order to gain an objective view on what is being expressed. For me often this is the only way to gain perspective on the feeling I'm having. It lets me shift myself out of being "in it" and into the realm of interacting with another person who, probably, feels grounded and sane in that moment and can reflect to me what is really going on with me.

When I found myself doing this work with clients all over the planet I realized that I was doing something interesting. It turned out that it wasn't useful just for me but was in fact needed by many. The benefits to my clients were real and often immediate, helping them gain perspective on a part of the self creating havoc, opening the door to compassionate self-acceptance, and learning to take back control of their lives from subpersonalities. Prior to this my own process had me wondering at times if talking to myself like that could be an indicator of a mental or emotional health issue or the opposite of health. At times early in the process of explaining this vision to clients to whom I was teaching it I caught myself seeming to describe what we might think a schizophrenic might experience. I was sure to be quick to explain that getting grounded, being intentional, and always unfolding the process of learning about these inner parts of self with understanding and compassion keeps everything in realm of health and growth. Note that the 19 stories of my soul's other lives explored in this book came into my awareness over almost a decade – it is not to be a free-for-all in which you are invited to lose your mind by being overwhelmed in any way. The second-to-last chapter of the book, "A

Woman Who Lost Her Mind," describes another life of my soul in which the fear of overwhelm dominates and I believe it took almost a decade for me to become practiced enough at the integration process to be able to deal with and successfully work with that portion of consciousness. Maintaining the intention that all go smoothly and that you will do what you can handle and not overload yourself goes a long way to setting up how the process would work in your life should you opt to pursue this sort of healing and growth.

Why Bother?

Because we are energetic beings we carry the capacity to inhabit many different sorts of energetic states. We experience them as emotions and emotional states. Since we are yet to become fully aware of what it means to be and live as energetic beings we are not yet operating ourselves with conscious awareness. Instead of conscious operation we pick up, absorb, borrow, and try on for size others' energies and those lying around in our environments often without knowing what we are doing. Even when we are aware that it has happened we might not know how to clear out our fields so that we are no longer subject to these other energies.

That we carry our own and others' energies within us, react to their existence, and are triggered variously by external dynamics can lead to a tendency to be emotionally reactive and/or to fear dealing with energies and emotions.

This state is the opposite of consciously operating ourselves because we are reacting to something and not being sure how to do it better or not do it. As a result later we might try to limit our expression and this in turn can create distortion.

The first reason why the processes and work described in this book matter is that it enables a person to learn more about the ins and outs of how the self is wired energetically and, therefore, emotionally. Learning to work with our emotions in conscious ways is important so that we can feel more at home in our bodies and lives. If we go from reactivity to stuffing to distortion and then more reactivity – creating a cycle as most of us do to some degree and on some level on a regular basis – then we are essentially at the mercy of the energies we carry, which means the emotions that we feel. *If we do this we are sentient but not conscious.*

According to the ascended masters and other guides I work with becoming fully conscious of our energetic and emotional selves is a next step for humans in the evolutionary process. Human intellect and intelligence have blossomed and now it is time for our sensitivities and awareness of energy to catch up. Routinely I work with smart people looking to open up or learn to trust their intuitive selves. Their minds are so good at keeping doors shut and limiting the participation of their feeling centers in their lives and opening things up can be a struggle. Our minds are wonderful but they have access to only certain sources of information. Alone they cannot manage our lives as energetic beings because they don't know what to do when emotions surface with which we have not had prior experience. They also do not know how to handle recurring emotional states that they cannot understand linearly and logically. When it comes to emotions our minds are pretty much clueless! The heart and feeling centers working to guide the mind while we stay in and conscious of our bodies is the way to deal with these issues.

The second reason this work is important is that limiting and ultimately ending emotional reactivity in favor of conscious response matters. When I know my emotional triggers on the surface as well as those below it and I have some context for the kinds of human situations that can understandably lead to those feelings, I can accept that I am wired the way that I am. This leads to a reduction in reactivity and an increased ability to respond to situations that threaten to or do trigger our hot-button emotional issues. Doing this work transforms one's conception of and relationship to fear and therefore one's willingness to act and choose in self-interested ways that allow full expression of all energies naturally present within the self. All of this leads to a markedly higher quality of life.

For instance, you will read about my angry reaction to a cat who lived with me who wanted to come in and out of the house seemingly every 10 minutes (in the chapter "Two Slaves"). It would annoy anyone after a while (no matter how cute the cat) but I had a reaction out of all proportion to the situation at hand. If I don't know what is at the source of it – whether that event or dynamic is present in this life or not – then I will likely continue reacting when in the face of it and similar situations. If I don't understand anything about it beyond my angry reaction then I set myself up to be powerless to be anything but angry in the face of that kind of scenario in the future. Once I have the context of at least a kind of source of that reaction (even if I do not remember another life of my soul's on the Earth timeline) I can stay grounded and intentional in how I work with situations in which someone expects me to do something that I perceive is unfair or takes advantage of me. When I can stem the emotional reactivity related karmically to a Uranus-Mars conjunction in the 1st house square the nodal axis (this will be explained in several chapters below) then I can learn to respond in ways that work well for me and others. When I do this my life is better on numerous levels.

The Birth Chart and Karmic Analysis

November 8, 1972
4:16 am
Dover, Ohio, USA, Earth
From birth certificate.

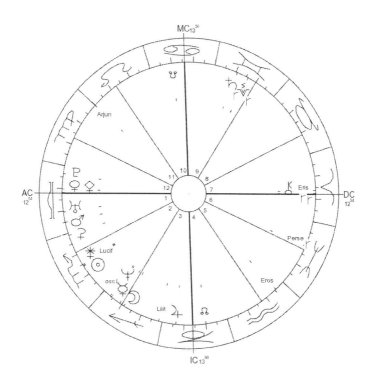

This chapter takes an objective view of my soul's journey via a karmic analysis of my birth chart using the 4-step process laid out and worked with in various ways in the first two volumes of The Soul's Journey series. As explained in those volumes the charts of the various humans as whom this soul manifests across the Earth timeline will not be identical. This is the chart of the one called Tom Jacobs who is born in Dover, Ohio on November 8, 1972 in Dover, Ohio and in other lives the charts of the individuals will differ. The major themes will be repeated in some way and the reader is advised to study the first two books in the series to gain a solid footing in this perspective before expecting to be able to fully grasp all that is contained below.

The analysis that follows can be taken as an example of how I prepare for any client reading as I study the themes in play given the 4 steps of the process. Going in to a reading with someone I've not met before and about whom I know nothing or next to it, this is the type of story about which I make notes. No matter what the person brings to me to discuss or understand more about in his or her life, this style of analysis provides the map of the soul's intended journey. When I speak with the person I get direct and indirect cues as to how he or she lives the chart but this kind of homework has proven invaluable to my work, enabling me to dial in to the core of an issue immediately. You will read in the remainder of the book about a variety of ways these themes surface in my life and no specific related to them could you predict by studying the chart alone.

First, here are the steps of the process. Each is considered in terms of house, sign, and aspects:[4]

1. Pluto represents the empowerment journey the soul intends that its human selves undertake and experience. Many experiences that leave the humans associated with the soul unfold that leave the person feeling confident, strong, and powerful and that life is worth living. Many experiences of the humans over the course of many lives leave them feeling less than confident and strong, or disempowered or powerless.

2. The South Node of the Moon (SN) represents the kinds of conditioning environments chosen by the soul for the humans including families to be born to and raised by. The SN tends to become a lens through which a person sees the world and expects the world to be, thereby creating a world around the self through karma/beliefs and vibration. The SN also represents habit patterns a person is attached to and a preferred comfort zone the person will be inclined to return to when stressed, challenged, or unclear how to proceed. This is a marker of what we do well due to having much

---

[4] When doing karmic analyses such as this one I tend to use 4th harmonic aspects (conjunction, square, and opposition) and quincunxes. No one has ever come in for a session from me complaining of a trine or sextile from Pluto to anything!

experience (whether we like it or not) and can often find a certain kind of success through doing.

3. The South Node ruler by sign (SN ruler) represents special skills, talents, and roles of this soul's humans in many lives. It can be that the humans show up with interests and passions related to this symbol or that others recognize that the humans can do things and appoint the people to certain roles and tasks. This is a layer of identity beyond and behind Sun, Moon, and Ascendant, typical markers of identity and personality most Tropical/Western astrologers look to first in chart analysis.

4. The North Node of the Moon (NN) as the opposite of the SN represents a blind spot or something that has been left out of the lives associated with this soul. It is opposite the person's comfort zone and habit patterns and therefore is a way of being and part of life with which the person is not only not familiar (because it has been left out of many lives) but also because it is the opposite of what the person prefers to experience. Often there are prejudices and biases that a person has about the NN such that they would never "want to be like *those* people." We need to learn to grow into this part of the chart and add it our repertory while not leaving behind the SN. Tempering the past (SN) with new information, perspectives, and tools (NN)

is the way we create balance and round out the soul's education through our human lives.

Pluto

Pluto in this chart is in the 12th house. It indicates that the soul's empowerment journey for its human manifestations will take place through the areas of life that have to do with the 12th house. These include surrender, exploring the nature of consciousness, escaping day-to-day reality, attempting to have a direct experience of the numinous and the cosmic mysteries, mysticism, and, ultimately, learning to align ego and sense of self with something bigger than and outside the self. Empowering experiences will include experiencing the self in some way as an integral part of the cosmic order and surrendering to a higher principle. Disempowering experiences will include feeling lost in the world or the universe and/or not welcome, overwhelmed by uncontrollable forces or mass movements, and powerless or unable to direct the course of one's life.

In Libra, this is happening through a lens of Venus. Fairness, justice, and harmony are important to this learning journey. It is likely that manifestations of this soul as humans will attempt to be empowered in the 12th house through one-on-one relationships because Libra is the sign of the other and the process of knowing the self through reflection. If the universe is the other then it might be personified at times as God. When the other is instead a person God-like status might be projected upon that other until the soul's manifestations learn to live in the 12th house in healthier ways through establishing a direct connection with the numinous. Empowerment with Pluto in Libra/12th can unfold through developing relationships that support further alignment with an outside truth to which the person can be aligned and therefore grow. It can also be in learning about life through adopting a universal conception of justice, harmony, balance, and fairness that transcends human conceptions of the same.

Here Pluto is conjunct Venus also in Libra/12th. This emphasizes the importance of relationship to the karmic journey of the soul. Venus from its Taurus symbolism also relates to values, skills, and resources including money and possessions. These will also at times figure prominently in the empowerment journey this soul's human manifestations undertakes. The addition of the asteroid Pallas Athene adds in a warrior-stateswoman energy as well as loyalty and creativity. This stellium including Pluto indicates that the empowerment challenges its human selves will explore include bringing the unseen parts of life belonging to the 12th house into conscious awareness through an exploration of relationships, values, skills, possessions, and creativity. At some times in many lives this exploration will yield positive results and at other times negative results – we can know this with certainty because the nature of the Pluto empowerment journey always includes highs and lows given the themes chosen by soul.

Jupiter in Capricorn/3rd squares Pluto. Squares to Pluto indicate something that brings friction, pressure, or criticism to what the human selves are doing in the spirit of becoming strong and confident when it comes to the Libran 12th-house Pluto. Jupiter in square to Pluto is about Jupiterian issues, situations, and others pressuring the empowerment journey of the humans associated with this soul. As Jupiter here represents situations, groups, and others associated with belief, faith, optimism/pessimism, and risk, we can know that this soul's human manifestations have encountered problems in many lives due to believing or not believing things, but also from and with others who do or don't believe things. Additionally this can represent scenarios in which the person will have the need to make a choice about where to fall regarding the optimism-pessimism fence. The square to Pluto from Jupiter speaks of at least a few instances in a number of lives taking a huge risk and it not panning out as hoped and planned. It also indicates that at other times it does pan out and the person feels successful. Which the person needs to deal with as a course correction in a given life (overly optimistic or overly pessimistic) will become apparent as the particular beliefs he or she is focused on in the present moment are revealed. (The current level of pessimism vs. optimism at any given time for this person cannot be seen from the chart alone.)

This is in the sign of Capricorn and so these risks can unfold over time. They can be the product of taking charge of something, being an authority figure of some kind, dealing with authority figures. Also it can be said that others who do Jupiter (belief, etc.) in a Capricorn way (solidly, firmly, responsibly, harshly, etc.) can be sources of friction for the person. In the 3rd house, risks and pessimism/optimism are sourced in learning, teaching, speaking, writing, and perceiving – when others bring this friction they are communicators, thinkers, teachers, and writers.

South Node

The SN is in the 10th house. This is a karmic journey in which the conditioning environments chosen by the soul for the person to be trained to be human have an emphasis on developing a public persona, reputation, career, and/or place in the world. Status, achievement, productivity, recognition, and respectability are important themes for any 10th house SN experiences. It is therefore safe to assume that work and ideas about the right role it should play in life occupy a prominent role in this soul's human lives. The family into which this soul's humans are born will have something important unfolding regarding work, ambition, status, and the right way to approach and live these parts of life. This SN placement is also about being perceived by the community in one way or another and so with a 10th house SN it is safe to assume that there is some sort of notoriety or fame/infamy in the family system, scale being relative.

The SN is in the sign of Cancer. This tells us that these public arenas of life are in these many lives considered and approached through the lens of Cancer – the lens of the Moon. Nurturing, mothering, caring, shepherding, and healing are some of the tools and motivations of this sign. We can expect that this individual has many lives of being part of a family system with this sort of reputation whether it is experienced as positive or negative. It also says that the reputation, respect, ambition, and level of being known by the public can be come with an emotional attachment for at least some of the members of the family system as the lunar archetype including the sign of Cancer indicates emotional and habitual attachment. And so it is that the work chosen and done and how it is received and perceived by others or society can inspire emotional attachment, too.

The squares to the SN tell a story of parts of life that the family system find in part confusing or vexing. All aspects to the nodes indicate life lessons the individual needs to learn but also that the family system needs to learn, too – they represent karma shared in common with the family system. Squares to the nodes say that a person knows something about expressing the energies in question but not enough to be happy, healthy, and successful with them. They describe certain habit patterns that are passed down through generations regarding which each member of the system is to one degree or another invited to learn to make new choices. Through relying on habits with these bodies square the nodes, the human manifestations of this soul can fail to learn to make new choices and expand their repertories and, often, feel that they go back and forth from shooting themselves in the foot and sticking a foot or two in the mouth. Not learning to make new choices with these energies leads to repeating past patterns and their accompanying missteps and blunders, which is true of various members of the family system.

Individuals with squares to the nodes can at times find themselves behaving in extreme ways regarding these energies as they seek to find the right expression. Exploring all possible expressions while keeping eyes, ears, and hearts open to observe the results and then make choices about what are the best kinds of expressions is key to creating balance and healing the karma associated with squares to the nodes.

Venus and Pallas Athene in Libra are square the SN from the 12th. Venus is about relationships and what is deemed to be fair, just, equal, and balanced, as well as creativity, self-worth, skills, values, and survival. In Libra this theme is emphasized and the combination says that creating equality in relationships is a confusing issue for the humans associated with the soul. Choosing the right people with whom to be in relationship and how to manage the ongoing business of living in partnership with others is important here. In the 12th house, relationships are experienced in a way that seeks to transcend day-to-day reality. There will be an element of spirit or the numinous that seeks to come out within and from relationships for this person. Venus in the 12th in Libra can at times get lost in idealization of spirituality, art/creative expression, beauty, or kindness and generosity. It is possible that the humans associated with this soul surrender (12th house) to beauty, attraction, etc., without remaining grounded and intentional about the kinds of relationships of which they are willing be part. Pallas Athene squaring the nodes is about karmic confusion when it comes to standing up for the self or others and it is also about creativity and loyalty being sources of vexation and choices that leave the person with the foot in the mouth or holes in that foot from shooting. Standing up for the self within relationship as well as standing up for particular relationships is something that needs to be explored in this life. Making sure that creativity is not sacrificed for the sake of loyalty to others is another possible theme.

Uranus conjunct Mars in Libra/1st are square the SN as well. Uranus represents freedom and individuation, inventiveness, objectivity, and breaking out of constriction of any and all kinds. Mars represents will, passion, desire, action, boundaries, self-assertion, self-defense, and rescue. There are many ways we can pair words from the lists associated with each of these planets but for now let's say that expressing free will and being free to individuate as the person desires have been karmically vexing issues over many lives. The chart holder will need to learn to express will, assertiveness, and desire in unique ways that set him free and allow him to be original. The right reasons for making self-interested choices might be confusing to this person because of the emphasis with several bodies in Libra square the nodal axis – new choices to set the self apart and put the self first should be learned by this person to cease repeating karmic patterns with these symbols.

Retrograde Chiron in Aries is square the nodes from the other side of the chart on the Descendant. Chiron square the nodes is about wounding and healing, dealing with suffering in self and other, and learning about managing one's energy to be healthy.[5] In the 7th house navigating these well within relationship can be confusing and challenging over many lives for the chart holder. There may arise issues about the inability to say "no" to others when their needs surface and this can result in sometimes inappropriate boundaries, responsibilities, and responses within relationships of many kinds. It is also true that this can result in the chart holder not asking others for what he wants, always being hypersensitive to how others might receive the request and, perhaps, expecting rejection for initiating relationship or activities within existing relationship. Another possibility might be to dominate or be assertive to the point of aggression to hide a sensitivity to the reactions of others. The sign of Aries is about boldness, passion, and behaving instinctively and one possibility is that wounded others (Chiron in the 7th) enter into the person's life and he is not clear about the right to say "no" to them or how to do it. That Chiron is retrograde says that the person must start from the ground up with a new way to approach relationship and all these

[5] See *Chiron, 2012, and the Aquarian Age: The Key and How to Use It.*

issues as old ways of doing them (and others' ways of doing them) simply will not work.

Eris in Aries/7ᵗʰ is next to the Chiron and is therefore also square the nodes. Eris is about having vulnerabilities and senses of inadequacies revealed by the words or deeds of another and how we deal with feeling raw and exposed. Many try to protect themselves by lashing out and many retreat inwardly to avoid conflict or making someone else wrong for their feelings. With Eris square the nodes in Aries/7ᵗʰ we can expect that the manifestations of this soul on many parts of the Earth timeline experience being a trigger and catalyst for others to become aware of their insecurities and vulnerabilities. In such situations what's happening is that a person is gaining insight into an unprocessed emotional knot, block, or bruise but the other person can, as mentioned above, be made wrong for being a catalyst. The humans associated with this soul are in the process of learning about how to deal with this in relationship. This could be said to be part of the boundaries module of these humans' Earth-bound education. The conjunction with Chiron says that other people's suffering is triggered by this person in various ways and the opposition to Venus-Pallas in Libra/12ᵗʰ indicates that often relationships are chosen and entered into in which insecurities and vulnerabilities play important roles whether this is positive and healing or negative and destructive.

Finally, the Ascendant-Descendant axis is square the nodes. This is about the definition of self and other that in each of us needs to come into and stay in balance through a regular process of taking time to express and be the self as well as be in relationship with others. The manifestations of this soul will have some karmic confusion about how to function independently as an individual as well as how to function as part of a relationship. Sometimes this can lead to not knowing what is whose responsibility and at other times it can lead to confusion about appropriate ways to respond to the requests, needs, and demands of others whether stated or implied. Saying "yes" and "no" to others for the right reasons at the right times represents important learning for this person and cleaning up the habitual responses while adding to the repertory of choices presents the opportunity for important karmic healing. It will open possibilities to be in relationships in new, healthy ways.

South Node Ruler

The ruler of the SN in Cancer is Moon. Moon in this chart is in the 3rd house in Sagittarius, part of a stellium with the true Black Moon Lilith, Neptune, and Mercury. The SN ruler in the 3rd house says that the various human manifestations of this soul show up for, take on, or are in different ways appointed to kinds of roles that relate to perception, writing, education, teaching, speaking, and other associated activities. The 3rd house relates to all parts of life in which information in-and-out figures prominently (education, communication, etc.). We can know that being someone trained by people who emphasize work (SN in the 10th house) we are looking at an individual who will in many ways gravitate toward writing, teaching, learning, and communicating as ways of being in the world. Sagittarius as the sign of the SN ruler adds to the story that this person in many lives carries strong faith, hope, and optimism as well as the opposites. A Jupiter-ruled SN ruler describes a person who is expansive in some way and, perhaps, takes up a lot of space (Jupiter being the largest body in the solar system aside from the Sun). The strength of beliefs in this soul's human manifestations will be strong as will the need for new information and experience to feed a deep sense of curiosity about life and, perhaps, anything or everything else.

The conjunctions to the True Black Moon Lilith, Neptune, and Mercury mean that the role these humans create for themselves, inhabit, or are appointed to have Lilith-like, Neptunian, and Mercurial qualities. In other words, this person will show up as a Lilith-Neptune-Mercury, Sagittarius/3rd house sort of figure in many lives. Because of certain environmental factors at some times it won't be possible for the person to express these energies outwardly but they are nevertheless at the core of the person's identity and sense of self in a large number of lives. Neptunian people can be dreamy, mystical, addicted, other-worldly, creative, and have faith in the bigger picture or grand plan. Mercurial people are communicators, critical, curious, talkative, and quick. Lilith figures are connected to instinct and can be erratic and unpredictable, and in some ways rebellious. The 3rd-house role this person inhabits and creates for the self (or is appointed to) features these behaviors and identities coming out in the context of learning, teaching, writing, speaking, etc., and in a Sagittarian way that can be big, grandiose, full of faith and hope or pessimistic, etc.

Moon is opposite retrograde Saturn and retrograde Vesta in Gemini/9th. The person in many lives will draw into his sphere authority figures (Saturn) dedicated to their beliefs and path (Vesta) who oppose him and have aims and methods that are counter to his. This can lead to challenges and confrontations at times and misunderstandings at others, often with miscommunication and false assumptions at the heart of the issue. There can often be tests of wills to see whose agenda can win out in the end. The experience will be of being blocked by Saturnian others (the normal experience of an opposition) while the soul's intention is that the humans associated with it learn to become appropriate Saturn (authority) figures while being challenged and confronted (opposition) by people who bring that energy. Given the SN ruler is in Sagittarius in the 3rd we can expect the opposition from Gemini in the 9th to have something to do with how this person knows what he knows. This can come in the form of fact-checking challenges and questions about the validity of what the chart holder is thinking, perceiving, saying, writing, and teaching or misinterpretations of it. One thing this can lead to in many lives is a mind that develops a useful openness and can clearly see potential objections to its own process and can also result in problems with authority figures but it can also pave the way for a person to have limited openness to the input of others given the critical nature from Saturnian others in many lives. Challenges and confrontations from Saturn-Vesta people can be heavy and unrelenting.

It is worth noting that the sign of the SN (Cancer) and its ruler (Sagittarius) are naturally quincunx. When looking at karmic stories this fact (as well as oppositions, squares, and inconjuncts – 30 degrees of arc) can simply and quickly explain a person who feels a bit of a black sheep when it comes to family, community, and culture. Quincunxes evoke a feeling of being unable to be in the same room with the other. While it is painful and at times confusing for the chart holder it is the soul's intention that the humans associated with it do not get stuck or complacent in the rhythms and ruts of the people to whom they are born while simultaneously providing inspiration for trying to find unique and novel ways to explore a state of belonging to a family even if the feeling of it does not bring much comfort or ease.

North Node

The North Node (NN) is in the 4th house in Capricorn. This is a part of life and a way of being that have been in many ways left out of the humans associated with this soul. These individuals will tend to emphasize SN styles of living and ways of being and Capricorn/4th house issues and modes will be left out by default at first. There will also be some prejudices in these humans about what it would mean, look like, require, and cost to live in the 4ᵗʰ house in a Capricornian way. They haven't done it after all and it opposes what they are familiar and comfortable with doing and being.

The 4ᵗʰ house is about home, family, nest, inner knowledge, the private parts of life, and committing to others for the long haul a la family and community. As the house of belonging and accepting others to be in our heart spaces and homes, parts of life here invite humans to build connections with others that will last and to which all parties are committed. Capricorn is about realism, the long-term, responsibility, structure, discipline, sacrifice, and doing something authoritatively. The combination of this sign and house with the NN here will lead the soul's human selves to confront the relative value of work, achievement, and recognition versus the benefits and rewards of inner knowledge, family, and home. All that each requires, offers, costs, and provides will have to be evaluated in numerous ways during these human lives. The ideal is for the person to learn in any given life to choose the new territory of the NN to augment the experiences associated with the SN that will be abundant in many lives.

At this stage of the analysis it is useful to compare and contrast some SN and NN activities and ways of being. I do this to make sure I can see clearly the challenges to the habit patterns, preferences, and comfort zones of the chart holder when looking at the NN so that I can adequately compare and contrast this for him or during the reading. Remember that the chart holder generally does not want to do the NN and might not warm up to the idea. He or she may cling to the patterns and ways of being that have grown out from overidentifying with the SN. One example of this person's preference (SN) is creating and performing work (10th house) and having an emotional attachment to the process and outcome (SN sign Cancer). The opposite (NN) is to look deeply within in mature, responsible ways (Capricorn) that reveal how the person really ticks (4th house). Too much emphasis has been put in many lives on the public self and learning to define the self in terms of how the public or society receives the person and his or her work. Whatever work is chosen by this person if there is to be emotional growth and sense of fulfillment by rounding out the karmic education (adding experience of the NN to that already carried related to the SN) then this person must allow it to reflect the new sort of identity developed by delving into his or her own inner emotional depths. Work and achievement must in some way become an extension of the person getting to know the self in a deep way.

A second example of this person's predilection related to the SN is to put work and status before emotional connections, which we could also describe as activity and achievement over maintaining heart-felt ties with others over time. In Cancer in the 10th house there can be rather immediate responses to one's efforts in the world while concerning Capricorn in the 4th, time and experience are needed to reap the rewards.

In the charts that follow you will see different karmic signatures in the birth chart highlighted in terms of the story or stories told in the chapter. You will see certain signatures emphasized a number of times in various chapters. To have many other-life stories related to particular configurations in one person's chart is entirely normal. It reflects that there are deep and impactful emotional dynamics in play in lives spread out along the Earth timeline that manifest the intentions of the soul.

Karmic Stories, Life Stories

A Youth

Covered in this chapter: Mars-Uranus in the 1st house square the nodal axis and Chiron-Eris in Aries/7th square the nodal axis.

I was living in Santa Monica, CA in 2006 when I hired a local hypnotherapist for a series of past-life regressions. More and more I saw that unexpressed anger was an active undercurrent in my life and it affected everything in my world. My choices in life seemed informed by anger or the denial or suppression of it and I knew I needed help to get to the bottom of it. I was practicing as an evolutionary astrologer at this point and incorporating spirit guidance in my readings and was familiar with some alternative approaches to getting at deeply-buried issues.

The hypnotherapist came to my office for each of the two sessions I had with him. In the first I wasn't sure anything was happening and he assured me that it was normal for the first time to not fully let go of control of the mind. He lead me on a meditation to I suppose open some channels up and that was that.

The second session was different. It was the first time that I had been taken into a hypnotic state yet was experiencing it as I observed it. I doubted that I could be aware of what was happening if it were really working. The experience was uncomfortable and I think part of me wanted to fight the surrender of control while another part definitely came forward to speak. This is normal for a 12th-house Pluto placement if the person fears losing control of the self or mind.

The practitioner lead me through a meditation that ended with finding myself in a life where anger is an issue. He asked me to look down at my feet to see what I was wearing and asked me some other questions. I was a male and my age was about 14. It came out that it was Denmark in the year 1284. He asked me to remember an event that was the source of my anger now. The situation that came up was one in which someone that boy knew had stolen something that belonged to him. It was unclear if it was a toy or a tool as the feeling fluctuated. I got the sense that this 14-year old wasn't the sharpest knife in the drawer and might have been a bit developmentally challenged, confusing a toy for a tool – it seemed to me a toy but he seemed to feel it was a tool.

A local boy a handful of years younger stole it and that youth became angry. This other manifestation of my soul lashed out at him, hurting him, and it was deemed all around unacceptable. He had not told his parents, hard working people who felt he was a handful and, it seemed, often had to deal with his outbursts and inappropriate behavior. He was ashamed for overreacting but also felt justified because he had been wronged and felt that no one cared if he was wronged. His parents were too busy and he didn't seem to matter to them except as a nuisance. Late one night soon after the father of that boy and some other men from the neighborhood came to the youth's house and took him, binding his hands and putting a hood over his head. The took him to the edge of town in a wooden wagon. They beat him senseless before throwing him with bound hands in a body of water to drown, to finally take care of the problem he seemed to be to everyone involved.

Now, I was watching this story unfold and did not in the least trust that it could possibly be the memory of a past life of mine. I could not fathom what nonsensical part of me was spinning a tale or why. The hypnotherapist had asked me to let go and trust what came up and I had tried to do so. As much as I could, I did. But at that time it did offer some answers. What kind of experience could lead someone to feel that his feelings don't matter, that life is unfair, and he might not be safe? Many different kinds of human story could provide insight and this certainly was one.

After a while I did trust the story as memory and began to see the thread in my field of a belief that no one cared about what happened to me or what injustice might unfold in my life. I saw my hesitancy to reveal my feelings and my experiences as I assumed that they didn't matter to anyone and, I had seemed to come to believe, that meant that my feelings themselves didn't matter at all. And I saw in it an example of my deep assumption that life is not fair and that anyone can do anything to me they want without consequence but if I react to anything there's some huge problem and, probably, copious quantities of painful blowback. With Mars-Uranus in the 1st house you might expect to find someone with a ton of physical energy and a healthy ego who will act upon it boldly and without apology. That they are square the nodes says that there are unresolved issues related to their expression and so I have had to learn to make new choices about self-assertion that won't get me into trouble, working to leave behind habits and assumptions about how the energies should be expressed. Extremes won't work in this life if I am to change the karma, which is to say that acting and lashing out will not help but also that being timid and afraid to stand up for myself won't either.

Most examples of being given opportunities in this vein (ahem, *tested*) came in school. In 1st grade the boy who sat behind me liked to bother me. One day he sharpened his pencil to the finest point and poked me in the back of the neck, angling the move so that teacher at the front of the class couldn't see it. What she saw was me turning around and exclaiming something in that boy's direction, which of course resulted in a note sent home to my mother. That was at age 7 and I really did not feel that I had the right to stand up to anyone. Things that were unfair felt weighty, too.

I "retaliated" a few times when wronged at other ages and some of those times found me in a bit of trouble as a result. At age 10 a girl who picked on me during recess received several requests from me to leave me alone and then a final warning, ignoring all of them. After more of the same she finally received a single punch in the arm like no 10-year old had ever meted out before. I remember being in the principal's office shortly after this being told that we do not hit people and replying that she had it coming. The man was kind and generous and I didn't want to give him trouble but I insisted that she deserved it after how she treated me and the numerous requests I made that she stop. I felt justified and he couldn't agree but I didn't routinely have behavior issues and so there was little more he felt he needed to do.

I admit that when this sort of thing happened as a teenager I had a bit of a smug response to the authority figures telling me I should not do such things. In 10th grade during a period of a bit over a week I found myself being hit on the head as I passed through a particularly congested hallway in the school. Two otherwise separate buildings had been joined with this after-thought walkway and it was narrower than any other halls. I was being hit by people who were taller than me and I could hear their laughter as they did it. On the second to last day it happened I caught sight of the kid who was doing it. The next day I put my trombone mouthpiece in my pencil bag and went to class, letting it hang loosely in my hand by my side. Such mouthpieces are molded metal tubes with some weight and are thick and dense at one end. The last thing you want to do is drop one on your foot or have one fly at you. When I felt myself hit on the head that last day I responded with my own, landing it squarely on his head with a thud as the metal made contact. Immediately I went to my music locker and put the mouthpiece back in the instrument case and then went to my next class.

It wasn't long before I was called in to the vice principal's office to answer for it. The other boy, two years ahead of me, was there. The man asked me if I had hit this other kid on the head a bit ago and if so why I had done it. I explained what had been happening for a week and what I did (without the mouthpiece bit). I said I had hit him back after over a week and with my pencil bag. The boy said with a whiny anger that it was hard and it really hurt.

The vice principal asked him if it was true that he'd been hitting me and the boy said he had. Then he asked to see the thing I hit him with and I happily handed over the 7-inch long, lightweight, leather zipped case containing a few pens and pencils. The vice principal looked at the boy like he was an idiot and told me I could go back to class. I felt smug in getting away with it and now, years later, I can see that in some lives I don't. Acting out in such ways with Mars-Uranus in the 1st house as part of a karmic pattern can have others retaliating to your retaliation. Things can escalate until there's all out war, even over something relatively minor. Bruised egos and needing to know one has the right to stand up for the self can be a troublesome combination for people learning to step back from extremes, as the conjunction square the nodes indicates that I have needed to do.

Astrologically, we might say that my Scorpio "cunning" took over instead of reacting instinctively with overt anger (Mars-Uranus in the 1st). Not that what I did was necessarily okay but at the time I felt I needed to do something to get back at those jerks. In the years since then I've noticed that I have a fear of reacting to being bullied in whatever form because I have a concern I will do damage and then be damaged as a result. There have been times when I've wondered if in the next moment I'll have to do something defensive with that Mars-Uranus and I do fear that my response will be entirely out of proportion to whatever is happening. There is an extremity of reactivity if that Mars-Uranus conjunction is not checked and worked with actively. The square to the nodes indicates that extremes of reactivity without thinking are possible and that I need to curb reactivity to change the karma.

In later years I was the recipient of two death threats that resulted from trying to get coworkers to do their jobs so that I could do mine. One occurred in a hotel kitchen in which I worked just out of college. I didn't want to get stuck in sealed offices with fluorescent lights to destroy my spirit so I worked in a few restaurants the first two years out of school. I was on the wait staff at the hotel and the man was a cook. It was a battle of wills with me asking him to do his job and him refusing until I phrased my request in such a way that seems to have inspired him to pick up a knife and run after me with an earnest, maniacal scream that he was going to kill me. I slipped into a conference room rather deftly but was tweaked on adrenaline – I have no idea how I was able to stop running once in the conference room and not freak out. He was suspended from work but it didn't feel like enough. There was nothing else I felt I could do. Eventually he apologized to me with his tail between his legs, truly embarrassed for how he had behaved. I took his hand and forgave him, which made him happy, but I had become so accustomed to ignoring him in and around the kitchen that my behavior didn't change. He was bothered by this and I think I got off a little on it. There was nothing I could do assertively to get back at him (I felt) and that passive-aggressive thing served as a stepping stone for me to know that I did in fact have the right to do something about how others treated me.

The other instance was when I worked in a hospital in Boston. I worked for some engineers and was to get a package for one of them by a certain time so a key piece of medical equipment could be repaired before being used. The other man worked in the receiving department didn't want to get it for me, the only way I would have been able to get the package. I believe it was just because he didn't like me and I in time phrased my request in such a way that seemed to inspire him to pin and tower over me in an elevator, literally slobbering and drooling on my person as he growled out the words that he was going to kill me. Again, I left full of adrenaline and called my boss. The man was suspended and again I didn't think it was enough. I had been wronged and didn't feel I had the right for appropriate recourse. I wanted to react violently to being threatened, which would have been an example of the extremes with Mars-Uranus in the 1st square the nodes. I wanted to bust out of my normally-controlled self and show him who he was dealing with! But I know it would have been awful and there are no regrets.

I don't usually react strongly to others' anger even if directed at me. In recent years however I've found that trying to deal with old anger under the surface does make me more reactive than I'd like to be. Most of the times as a kid when I did defend myself were when my sister picked on me and did uncool things to make my life harder. She seemed to thrive on making me suffer. She got hurt a few times as a result but I always asked her several times to stop before warning her and long before reacting physically. Maybe that's what you get when you have two kids with fixed, 2nd house Suns squaring each other! Hers is in Aquarius and mine's in Scorpio.

If nothing else that 2nd hypnotherapy session helped me understand more directly that the source of all anger is pain and that some pain that I have carried is sourced in feeling stepped on by life. In that particular life described above it was a group of men who kidnapped, beat, and ultimately left the young man to drown but in this life all the bad things that have happened have seemed to be messages from life itself. If bullies abuse you and no one's looking out for you, it can seem like life is condoning if not causing it. I am not fully clear on whether that youth felt that way but that is something I saw about me now that was instructive and a benefit from that session.

The plan was for three sessions but I couldn't follow through. At the time I was fully weirded out by the feeling of a voice emerging from within me that was not my conscious mind. Since then I've channeled a number of different beings and am comfortable choosing to allow certain others to speak through me when it works for me but at that stage I was not in the least comfortable with anything of the kind. It was weeks if not months before I was interested in thinking about the session and it was a handful of years of other experiences – such as those you'll read about below – before I fully trusted what had come through.

Another detail that made sense in time was that the youth had been hooded prior to his death by drowning. When I was a kid I swam well and had no fears of the water but have always had a problem having my head and face covered. Fears of suffocation would come up but since I usually avoided having anything on or near my face it didn't come up that often. And then I took a safety course through a motorcycle training organization and it was the first time I put a motorcycle helmet on my head. We were standing in a parking lot preparing to learn to operate a motorcycle and were told to pick out a helmet that would fit. I put one on and started to cry, doing what I could to stave off panic. Immediately I removed it and tried to get a sense of what was happening but wasn't sure. I was going to have to put it back on to get on a bike and decided to just let the feeling be. The first minute or so was awful and then I just decided that I'd deal later with whatever the source of it was. During the over years I've owned and ridden motorcycles it's come up a few times as an issue but I've become more able to work through fearful feelings like that by getting grounded and deciding that I am safe. A few times I cried through it, letting the fear come to the surface, letting it be what it is, and telling myself kindly that it's alright that that was happening but that I would have to wear a helmet if I were going to ride a bike. In the end it's come out as a generalized feeling that I prefer not having a helmet on my head which just means that the first thing I do after getting off the bike is to remove the helmet. I've always preferred fresh air and felt a little stifled when I can't have it and this seems to fit with that more now than a panic about the possibility of suffocating when something is on my head.

In the years since that session I've had numerous opportunities to learn about and deal with the anger that inspired me to work with the hypnotherapist in the first place. Many angles have been needed to begin to understand the full picture and I'm in the process of changing some deep beliefs that inspire anger. Some of the experiences detailed below will add to the picture of old anger that comes up in my life now and I feel fortunate to have a number of experiences that have helped shed light on the issue.

A Former Monk

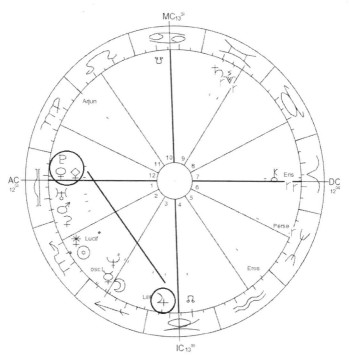

Covered in this chapter: Pluto in Libra/12th square Jupiter in Capricorn/3rd.

This story was uncovered after setting out to understand threads of pessimism, hopelessness, and despair I had carried with me for as long as I could remember. They surfaced a bit more often than periodically and, sometimes, ruled the day. I have a strong optimistic side that can be not just neutralized by my strong pessimistic side but in fact crushed to the point of feeling beyond repair. I always come out of it but it has been known to take Herculean effort, months, or both. The damage to my quality of life and relationships over time called for looking into it.

I remember that this came up in a session I was having with an intuitive though I do not remember which one. I've done a number of trades with colleagues over the years as well as had paid readings and this other person's particulars escape me now. We were discussing my refusal to have faith in life, the Universe, and God and the practitioner got the image of a monk wondering, "why me?" That brought imagery rushing forward for me: *On foot in the woods, barefoot with feet damaged by days of walking. It is rainy and cold and seems like it couldn't get much worse. The head is shaved in the middle in the style of a monk and a well-worn brown cowl covers the body. The emotion is deep pain at feeling let down and abandoned by God and anger has given way to sobbing.*

I felt into whether this monk had been kicked out of a monastery or had left of his own accord and then the bereft feeling come to dominate. Since then as I've revisited this part of me – the image calls up the feeling that exists within me, the bleed-through that is always with me – and it seems to me now as I feel into him that he left the monastery out of despair and it could have in the end been a mutual sort of thing: he lost faith in God and those in charge at the monastery could have given up on him because he had thoroughly chosen to give up on God. I don't get the sense that there was animosity but that because the man had admitted giving up on God and being unable to have faith that there was nothing further the brothers could do for him and the decision was made that he should leave.

Jupiter square Pluto can draw life experiences to one in which he risks everything on faith and then finds out he was wrong. It can also be in general a huge bet or gamble that sometimes works out and sometimes does not. With Pluto in the 12th and Jupiter in the 3rd, it seems that learning and/or thinking something pressured (the effect of a square) the 12th-house mission to find the truth. This can be a signature of established doctrine (Jupiter in Capricorn) overshadowing the need for higher answers and a direct connection with the divine (Pluto in the 12th). It can also be a signature of making a promise upon which one cannot deliver when it comes to keeping faith in the face of facts revealed. In other words, hope and faith can be dashed against the rocks when one learns what is said to be in the mind of God or how life unfolds differently than the call to faith seemed to imply.

I've been able to connect this life story and its associated emotions with (his) memories of perceiving that he had done all that God had asked and still been abandoned. In Christian lore figures have been known to be tested in their faith in God and this former monk perceived he was not able to measure up to those in scripture who, when tested, chose to endure anything. He feels he doesn't have it in him to sacrifice everything but needs a connection with the divine. He also feels that being tested to the point of deep suffering is entirely unfair and a cruel trick – he sees God as a mean-spirited trickster.

I don't know what he experienced specifically that left him fully unable to have faith. I suspect it has to do not with a personal loss such as the death of someone important (an experience that has tested my faith in numerous lives) but a general sense of seeing how the world works and that being in conflict with doctrine, what is taught to the religious and is meant to explain the will of God and therefore the state of the world. For example the notion that man is fundamentally flawed and born a sinner doesn't make sense to this man but I can feel that he tried to work within doctrine and adapt his thinking to what he was told is the truth. As I sense into him now I can identify crises of faith that ended up overwhelming his attempts to align with what he was told is the will of God. Too much of reality made no sense in the face of the manifest world for him to be able to maintain faith in that god described in that doctrine.

By today's standards perhaps we could say he became depressed. My sense is that it lasted for years – even up to a couple of decades – and that he worked diligently to put off his doubts and concerns while continually focusing on the teachings and doctrine which were part and parcel of his calling. To feel called to serve God in that way and then to find inconsistencies that seem to indicate that God is not worth following or respecting can lead one to doubt the entirety of his life mission. In the end he was unable to persist in living with the tension between what he was told was true and what he found to be true.

This story parallels my own relationship with spirit guides. How they view our lives and as a result advise and guide us can sometimes lead us into difficult scenarios in which we'd rather not find ourselves. They approach us in loving ways but often the thing we need to do is confront pain from the past in order to heal some knot, block, or bruise we still carry that holds us back or limits us. If we assert that we want to head in one particular direction they will in fact help us but often this can come in the form of pointing out to us how and why we block ourselves from getting there. We have to face and heal pain to progress, as it happens.

This point is a critical one I teach to my students and use with my clients on a regular basis and yet does represent an ongoing issue I have with my guides (ahem, *that I have with me and my thought process*). There is a stack of evidence parts of me collate and present when asked to have faith that what's coming down the pike is helpful even though it just looks like some kind of unfair crap storm. There is a part of me that is indeed capable of having faith in the process and that my guides are here to help me but it is part of my life learning to confront resistance that other parts of me carry about trusting life, the universe, Goddess, God, and guides. When I recall the former monk's memories I become acutely aware of the depth of despair that a human can get himself into and grind himself down by if he lets it happen.

This life story reminds me that we have a choice in how we see the world. Specifically this man was not trained to ask the right questions about who this god is and what it wants because of the man's surroundings and conditioning. In my life I have access to all sorts of metaphysical teachings that are based in something other than religion but this man did not. In many centuries on Earth in the last 6,000 years if you wanted to be educated you ended up getting involved in religion. For chunks of time Christian monasteries were where books and therefore knowledge survived through the Dark Ages. Major universities began as religious institutions in many places, before there was a paradigm of science that was based in something other than religious faith (or fervor).

Religions can serve as vehicles for spiritual exploration, of course. If however we get stuck at the limits of doctrine we can fail to see beyond it, leaving us attempting to reconcile ideas of what is happening with what we observe to be the truth of what is happening. We can look at this astrologically as seeking Neptune or experience in the 12th house (related to Neptune) and getting stuck with Jupiter or in the 9th house (related to belief). With my Pluto in the 12th house it's critical that I explore spirituality but with my Saturn in the 9th house I can tend to get stuck with an idea of what spirituality is and entirely miss the boat for the clever machinations of my wily human mind. And Jupiter in Capricorn in the 3rd house squaring Pluto can describe karmic scenarios of getting stuck in a rut and hemmed in by the limits of doctrine, too. Each human can go through such a process though not all at the soul level need to do so frequently. With the birth chart signatures mentioned here the volume on this life theme is turned up in my journey.

Now I have the choice to question and to seek answers that fall outside what religion can offer. As you'll read more about below in the chapter "Three Church Men," this life for me seems in part about deconditioning from religious indoctrination over the course of many lives so that I can experience something that feels truly true; so that I can leave behind mind-based assumptions of what must be true in favor of energetic/vibratory resonance of what I sense is true. Any human who is observing reality and is unhappy with at least some portion of it may come into contact with parts of the self that resist having faith in life, the universe, Goddess, God, et al. It's one of the major human evolutionary steps necessary for our growth and yet it requires adapting to a view of ourselves as life, the universe, Goddess, God, et al. – our lives are not happening to us but are creations of our souls intended to teach them about using and dealing with the results of free will and what love is, where it comes from, and who is responsible for giving it to whom.

In my case I am in a long-term process of making peace with the difficult creations of my soul and my human choices in deciding what those experiences in religious contexts in various lives have meant. A lot of people live such a journey and it's just what I'm focused on these days perhaps more than some other people. I know that I am making progress (being able to put all of this into words without charge – including the human- and soul-based perspectives that can radically differ – spells progress to me) yet I am still in process with this. I have days during which I feel like that bereft, depressed, agony-filled former barefoot monk wandering aimlessly in the rainy, cold forest and looking up to the heavens with deep sorrow and wondering, "why?" But I also have the ability to see other perspectives on those feelings, get grounded, and consciously work with the parts of me (including those anchored in other parts of the Earth timeline) that leave them feeling heard, respected, and able to proceed with me running the show.

With other-life parts that come forward with intense feelings such as this one it can be easy to get lost in the emotion. It is simple to just give in to the pain or anger – it's seductive, really. For some reason we can tend to choose either to resist the rush of emotion (leading to rigidity and a closed emotional center) or give in fully and be washed away by the feelings. I offer that you can create a middle road: Learning to work consciously with emotions by first getting grounded and then actively managing the parts within you while staying compassionately in charge. As a collective we are in the process of being exposed to and learning about ourselves as energetic beings. This will take us out of being available to be swept away by our emotions and take us into being able to participate in our emotional natures and dynamics as conscious creators. These days this is the bulk of my work with clients.

So, yes, it is true that I carry these feelings and it is true that they are anchored in another part of the timeline in the form of other humans associated with my soul. But it is also true that I'm supposed to be the one running my life! The only way to reconcile this is to admit complexity and introduce tools designed for conscious management of that complexity.

A Man Who Would Cherish a Woman

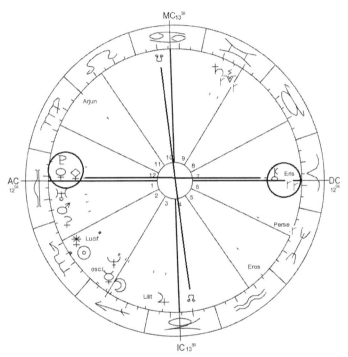

Covered in this chapter: Pluto-Pallas-Venus in Libra/12ᵗʰ, Chiron in Aries/7ᵗʰ opposing Venus in Libra/12ᵗʰ with the pair square the nodal axis.

At a Hellinger Family Constellation group meeting I met a woman I could feel from across the room. During the sessions that night all I noted about her was that she was attractive and seemed kind but after, when people were mingling, I could sense her energy and was piqued. I had never done anything of the kind before but I sent out cords from my heart to draw her to me – I just had to get closer to her and with all the conversations happening left and right I wasn't sure how to make that happen. (It did not occur to me to just drop what I was talking about go over to her! The feeling of wanting to be close to a stranger made me nervous.)

In a few minutes A. made her way to me and we talked. After some talks on the phone and meetings over the next few weeks a relationship was underway. Each of us felt a multilife connection though at first neither of us had a sense of details or purpose. We happened to share the idea that relationships come about for a reason and often it can be to resolve something from the past but neither of us knew at that time what might need to happen between us to resolve things.

One day at the beginning of the shift from hanging out to being involved with each other, A. did have a sense of a situation from another life that was unresolved between us. I cannot now remember the words and images and all I retain from that day as regards that conversation is that I felt relief that she recognized me and that I felt safe with her and so very happy to be with her. I have a vague memory of her telling me, "I'm here – I'm with you," and feeling a great sense of relief as I balled my eyes out.

But what I want to tell you about is the sense that came to the surface in me as time went by. I remember distinctly putting words to it after we moved in together a few months into the relationship. Feelings of total adoration bordering on worship came up in me and I'm not sure I'd felt love in that way – or modified with those other things – before. It didn't feel weird but that it was a complete opening of my heart. A. didn't mind feeling worshipped because it was authentic and not manipulative or strange but I knew there was something in there for me to unearth about the connection in other lives. At some point I realized that in at least one other life I had loved her from afar and craved the chance to be with her. I came to see that in that other life she was essentially the property of a rough and unkind man and I ached as I saw her treated as property and abused. From my viewpoint her husband in that life was abusive and controlling but not everyone could see that. They saw that he had means and outfitted her in splendid clothing and enabled her to shine as an attractive woman, something valued in that cultural context. I had the sense of seeing her on a regular basis but not being connected to her family or household in any particular way. It felt as though when I saw her in that other life it was in public. I sensed that we had not had direct contact but that our eyes had met and, of course, that she had no idea that I pined to be with her. With A. in this life I began to have the thought repeatedly come to the surface, "If only she were mine …" And while she wasn't mine to own she was choosing to be with me. I was fine with the distinction and so I knew it was a thread from another life. This was an important point in my process to integrate and heal issues unfolding on other parts of the Earth timeline because in the other life I had been bent out of shape because I couldn't have something important to me. In this life I had it and I realized that the other-life me was wrong – it wasn't in this moment lacking, there was nothing missing. I absolutely did get to be with her! A big part of the healing was recapturing the sense that the love I have to offer matters.

Pluto in Libra can indicate a deep sense in a person that other people are needed for the individual to be able to become empowered. It is the sign of the other and those in this generation (the births from 1971-2 to 1984) put a strong emphasis on the existence, presence, and reflection of others. At times this can get specific and a particular other can be appointed to be the one to help the chart holder be strong and confident. People in this astrological generation can get hung up on relationships in this way, waiting for another or a particular other to be want to be with them. Pluto in this sign is an indicator that the soul intends its humans to learn about fairness, harmony, balance, equality, and other things through relationship. This is true of all humans but this group of people have the volume on this need turned up so loud that much else can be drowned out as they try to meet the need.

Adding Venus in Libra to Pluto emphasizes the role I can put on relationships in my various lives. With Pallas Athene also here there are a couple of different threads that occur to me to weave in. One is loyalty and it would add to this that when various mes get interested in someone there can be a bit of fixation on that person and the potential relationship or, if it happens and ends, memories of being with that person. Another thread is trying to divorce the self from the Venus-Pluto in Libra energy for some reason. "Attempted divorce" is a thread I use with Pallas as in order to be successful in her world and taken seriously as a woman, she felt she had to deny that she was born of a woman – she had to deny her matrilineal heritage, an obvious negation of an important part of herself.[6] In the 12th house this story involves grand and idealized feelings, longing, and at times loss. The combination of these three symbols in this configuration can lead in various lives to longing for love relationships. The heart can open wide and deep and yet in the 12th house things don't always go as planned. Actually they rarely go in any way remotely related to a human's plan! Venus square the nodes from the 12th can also be an indicator of not speaking up to others about my feelings about them. This has happened in this life, certainly.

Speaking of that, Chiron-Eris in Aries/7th are also square the nodes and deserve mention in this context. Normally Aries/7th behavior seeks to be direct, honest, and bold in relationship and can quickly initiate relationship based on instinctive desire and knowing. With Chiron here there can be in the chart holder a sense of potential rejection everywhere he or she turns as well as a tendency to find Chiron in other people. As Chiron indicates wounding and healing, these are prevalent in relationship

---

[6] See *Living Myth: Exploring Archetypal Journeys.*

for such a person but given the place in the karmic story due to being square the nodal axis, there is confusion about all that Chiron represents. This can manifest as an unwillingness to ask others for what one wants as well as being afraid to make contact with other people for fear of rejection. Adding Eris to the story brings in the element that asking others for what one wants or initiating relationship can stir up others' insecurities. The result can be that I might tend to withhold my feelings and desires from others – and in fact hide them – for fear of being rejected because I always somehow stir others' issues when it comes to desires and feelings. In the context of this other-life story, of course I wouldn't approach her in that other life! She belonged to an abusive man and she was out of my league. Now, what I would have defined as my league would have been informed directly by a fear of rejection by others (a lack of self-confidence) and perhaps not being sure how to ground and bring into concrete reality all of the 12th-house feelings that can be inspired by Venus-Pluto in Libra in that house.

When we met in this life, A. was looking for the right man to begin having a sexual relationship. She had clear ideas about what the right kind of dynamic would look like but was not specific – it was about an energetic and emotional dynamic and from what I could tell had to do with the quality of interaction between her and a man. When we met she was actively looking for a relationship and I was a handful of days out of a brief relationship that had not gone smoothly. In the end of that prior one I asked the universe to inspire me in some way. I was shocked out of that other space with inspiration upon meeting A. and she had my attention – and she wanted it.

I had the sense that being with this woman was a privilege and I was overflowing with happiness for the opportunity to be with her. I had the chance to love her while being in relationship with her and I did cherish that time. It was an opportunity for me to learn to work more consciously with both Venus-Pluto in Libra/12th – how to feel in grand ways that could be grounded and not idealize the other – and Chiron-Eris in Aries/7th – the relationship offered chances for healing for each of us and I was able to work more consciously with what I wanted as well as ask another for those things.

One of the major themes in her soul's journey has to do with learning to create relationship that offer structure yet also freedom, space, and/or elbow room. Her chart screams that her soul has other lives on Earth in which she at times feels trapped in the wrong relationship and might not feel strong enough to break free while at other times might avoid being in relationship to avoid the possibility of losing freedom. Control and domination are themes in her soul's journey that her human selves need to unwind and release. We talked about those themes from time to time and she found it challenging to learn to take up the right amount and kind of space – this was her first sexual relationship and first time living with a man with whom she was involved.

When A. told me she had to leave me and our home I was broken-hearted and didn't know what to do. During that conversation I didn't fight her on it and she thought it was odd. But I asked her, "Wouldn't you prefer that I take you seriously, that I respect what you're saying?" I think she knew how attached I was to her and she was aware of the life story from the other part of the timeline that had me pining for her there. (She had gotten to know that Venus-Pluto in the 12th pretty well!) She therefore anticipated a lot more resistance to her decision to leave than she received. It wasn't easy at all but we had almost another month as she found a place and got organized to move. We were able to spend time together during those weeks and resolve things. It was a difficult month and I did have a hard time letting her go but I did what I could to respect that that was what she needed.

At some point during that month we had a conversation in which something clicked. I think it was the culmination or ripening of what it was that I needed to do for her in this life from the perspective of our soul agreement. We were standing in the kitchen talking and after a hug and me telling her that I loved her, I looked in her eyes and told her never to settle for less in a relationship than being worshipped. I said that she should never settle for less than being respected and adored. She got it and for me the moment resonated deeply. I didn't have a sense that we were complete but years later, I can see that she needed her first relationship to be spectacular. Her soul intended that she come out of lifetimes of other kinds of treatment and hit the relationship ground running in this life with a man who treated her like royalty, as a precious being, with kindness and respect, and who cherished everything about her.

What I haven't mentioned is that there was an age difference that some noticed, including me at the beginning. About 15 years separated us. It didn't often seem that that was the case and some friends have reflected to me that I was perhaps emotionally 15 years behind my chronological age. At the time it offended me but I get it now. From the souls' perspective, however, that difference in age was necessary. I had a level of experience in relationship and she was just ready to begin chapters of her adult relationship life when we met – it was a setup for me to teach her something about relationship that can only be gained through living it.

Cherishing A. and treating her in all the warm, kind, celebratory ways I couldn't in that other life when seeing her from afar freed something up in me that has turned out to be critical to who I feel I am. When we split up one thing I found difficult was owning my sensual side since she had brought it out so effortlessly. It's another feature of living with Pluto-Venus-Pallas in Libra/12th and Chiron in Aries/7th – some desires of yours are hidden and not clear (12th) and others you fear will get you rejection (7th). Before meeting her I wasn't sure how to access the lover in me and some of the women I had been with in prior years had trouble finding the right ways to connect with me and me with them. At this point in my life the lover is present and ready to go – ready to show love when I feel it and not hold back. That of course can bring up other issues but this relationship opened the door for me to reconnect with my own inner lover and to flow from the heart without as many barriers based in belief that my feelings and desires don't matter.

Two Men Who Will Do Anything to Achieve Their Goals

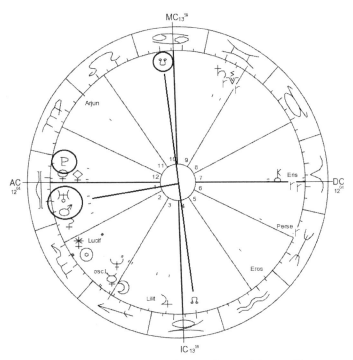

Covered in this chapter: 10ᵗʰ house SN and Mars-Uranus square the nodes, Pluto in Libra.

Whatever That Thing Was, He Did It With Conviction

Before we moved in together A. lived in a condo community that had a sauna. I went over one time and we used that special hot room – one of my favorite things – and were talking about an aspect of my personality that didn't seem all that useful at the time. It was a part of me who sees things in simple, black-and-white terms. When he makes up his mind he does not change it for anything. Up to that point I had joked that I had a little totalitarian running around inside me but that day I ceased being able to joke about it.

We were discussing how there are certain things about which no one could reason with me and certain times when I seemed utterly to lack compassion. In trying to get to know and love that part of me over the years I had worked with the idea that maybe it was a plus because this part of me had standards and was willing to work hard to get something done that was important to him. I admit to being in general more rigid in my opinions and less compassionate all around up to a couple of years after this incident. It seems I had to work with the St. Germain side of the ascended master I channel a lot more and live some of his ideas as baselines in my life in order to open my heart more and edge away from the edgy black-and-white part of me.

During this conversation A. seemed to be casual when she said, "Well, maybe you were a Nazi." Immediately I was incensed and didn't know what to do. I wanted to lash out at her but it had been said and I couldn't change it. Instantly I did the mental math on the fact that she did know me well and that it was possible she could reveal this about me to others but that even if she didn't it was still a problem that she had that view of me. This part of me insisted to me that I/we had done a fantastic job of seeming nice, good, kind, generous, and likeable and that obviously something along the way had failed – something had been sloppy or left out and the façade hadn't worked. A SN in the 10th house can have a person over many lives concerned about how others esteem him. It has to do among other things with reputation and being seen by others or a community as a symbol of something done in the community or world.

The grounded and centered part of me was during this exchange observing everything. It was amazing! The grounded and centered part of me was already pretty clear I have not lived a life as a Nazi but that perhaps something else similar in another part of the timeline has been experienced. Later I learned that the life as a writer described below took place during the World War II and so unless there are parallel soul manifestations (which I did not believe then but now I sense that there probably are – I have not been educated about that yet and have not meditated on it thus far) then I couldn't have lived a life as one of those Nazi people.

More than the specific the label "Nazi" it was the notion that I was evil. This me somewhere else on the Earth timeline is so dedicated to his goals that nothing will stop him. The irritations of blocks to goals and the inconvenience of other people getting in the way can be dealt with in many possible ways, he feels, and it is likely that due to his commitment to those goals his moral compass at times doesn't have 360 degrees. In the end I know it's just one way to live a life as a human and I have learned the power available through choosing compassion for people who do damaging things to others (even when it's me who has done that damage). We are each fumbling around trying to learn what it means to live human lives and we are all the Divine having forgotten that truth about ourselves. Because of this I recognize that the full variety of human experiences both through choosing to act and being acted upon are necessary for cosmic consciousness or All That Is to learn about itself on this complex, multifaceted, sometimes-inexplicable-seeming journey of life. Therefore I mostly no longer judge what most of us want to judge; I no longer think of evil in the same way. For me it isn't a threat of some foreboding awful thing but a choice that each of us has in every moment: to move toward what we know is good or to move away from it.

Mars in the 1st square the nodes describes a karmic journey of exploring the use of will and the experience of assertion and aggression. One angle on this with Uranus conjunct it adds an ability to detach and be objective. This can lead to using Mars in a state disconnected from the emotional impact of one's actions. That famous Uranian detachment can have a person doing without much care for the results. In me I see this occasionally as coming out when I'm willing to do something difficult that might hurt or cause problems. I can snap into a mode of willing myself to do it anyway and just walking into and through the experience in a very Uranian way. Of course this can be an asset but if your moral compass is missing some of those important degrees you might also find yourself able to justify doing things that don't seem or feel right.

Another angle on this is that in lives when we make choices that hurt others it is often because of perceptions and beliefs that we must do so in order to survive or to keep alive something we wish to keep alive. This could be life itself, a lifestyle, the status quo, an agenda of some kind, national, racial, ethnic, or religious identity, or anything else. Wars are the playgrounds of what we consider evil yet there is more going on. Look at the political justifications for and ascribed causes for wars of all kinds and you will observe people and groups perceiving that violence must be undertaken in order to survive or to protect something that is or is perceived to be alive and worth saving.

But this part of me – this man living his life on another part of the Earth timeline – most certainly does fear the judgment that he is evil, that what he is doing is not okay in the eyes of others and society. He is doing things that he feels to be justified in order to achieve his goals and create what is important to him. He seems to me to be at least sometimes working as though ends justify means. In this moment – how he comes through to me now – the activities and behaviors that could be called or are labeled "evil" are finished. He doesn't appear as someone ready to do anything but someone who has a past and is on edge about being found out by others.

The main issue with A. in that moment was that she could see him – he felt hidden and that he had been successfully passing himself/me off as kind, gentle, generous, etc. But suddenly she had made of herself a problem because she could see him and said something that indicated it.

I remember nearly foaming at the mouth because of this while observing his fear and near panic. I am not sure precisely what happened afterward but I sort of have a memory of storming out so she couldn't keep seeing into me. I seem to have gone out to the gym area for a few minutes before going back in to apologize and try to make nice with her. I don't remember how the situation resolved that day but I've been aware of that life thread from somewhere else on the Earth timeline since.

Whatever Needs Doing, He'll Do It Without Hesitation

Recently another persona with a similar vibe has come forward in response to a particular situation at home. Before my current girlfriend J. and I moved into the rental property on which we live as of this writing we asked the neighbors and property managers about the frequency and noise level associated with dog barking in the area. This was an issue in our previous residence and we knew for sanity and mental health we needed to live in a quieter place. I work from home and to be constantly having to shift my plans for recording and writing (and in general thinking) to wait out a fit of obnoxious barking was, at best, an issue. We were told it was not bad at the new place and this was a deciding factor in wanting to live here.

Once we moved in we realized that it was much more of a problem than was represented to us. Because I've been working so much the last few years I've spent the vast majority of my time at home, churning out books, MP3s, and teaching materials. There are times when I drop an ice cube into a glass or close the medicine cabinet in the bathroom as anyone would (not too hard, loud, etc.) and a dog starts barking. It can continue for hours with no apparent provocation, too. I don't blame the dogs but the owners who leave them outside too often and too frequently. We live in a city and while it's not wall-to-wall apartment buildings (many of us have yards in this area) our choices still affect each other. With the worst one I've called the police a handful of times to complain but it hasn't made a difference as far as we can tell.

There is a part of me that has made himself known during this process. Because I record quite a bit of material as part of my work between channeling, videos, and MP3 readings of different kinds the noise level surrounding the house matters. At perhaps the 25th or 30th time I had to put away the video camera or turn off the computer's microphone because of loud, hours-long dog barking, I realized that the simplest solution to the issue was to kill the barking dogs one by one.

With Pluto in Libra I do try to be a kind person and spread kindness in the world. Not that I am perfect by any means but this extreme thought stood out as something that was clearly part of me but perhaps not quite fully me. I tuned in over the course of days – which was far from difficult given that my anger at the situation surrounding me stirred this part of me up quickly and was a stark contrast to how I perceive I am normally – and listened to what he had to say.

Essentially this part of me is willing to do anything to have peace in order so that I can do my work efficiently and expeditiously. He is willing to go as far as to commit violence to the beings who seem to be standing in my way. At first I wondered if it is the other-life piece described earlier in this chapter but it has a decidedly different tone. This man is willing here and now to do what is necessary to achieve the goal. He is willing to do awful things to get what he wants. He would not apologize for it though he would do it in secret to avoid the complication of other people's fears and projections. The one described above had done some things that he was clear would (and perhaps should!) be considered awful by regular people and this one is in the present moment ready to such things. What is perhaps more disturbing than his suggestions and game plans to rid me of having to deal with this persistent noise is that he doesn't consider them bad things to do. He has a clarity about the importance of the goal – namely channeling and doing readings for people that will support them in healing and changing life for the better – and the detail that these dogs are living beings who perhaps shouldn't be caused to suffer is irrelevant. He co-opts some of my knowledge and terms when he replies that the souls of the dogs can't be damaged by killing them and that if they are incarnating to annoy the [expletive] out of people then they are incarnating also to learn about the myriad effects that can follow said annoyance – including being murdered as a result.

My strategy these days in dealing with angry and negative parts of me – that I know mostly through the arousal of anger and frustration – is to be with them, hear what they have to say, instruct them that I'm in charge of this life and I will welcome and value their input, and then proceed with making my own decisions whether they like it or not. This can take months to fully work through with some parts of consciousness (other-life selves) in part because some of these pieces of self are so uncomfortable to be around, witness, interact with, and let speak with my voice that I sometimes tend to limit my exposure to them. This can seem a good idea so to control the flow of anger such a part of the self can have but it ultimately draws out the process, making it much longer than it needs to be. In this case I gave in to hearing, thinking, and feeling all he has to say. I let this part of me devise the game plan for offing these dogs one by one (there are 7 on 5 different properties that trade off barking fits) and then laughed about the whole thing. I'm grounded enough to know I will not do the violent, offing things to the animals (or anyone else) but other parts of me do have some embarrassment at the level of willingness to do violence to achieve peace.

Pluto in Libra is all about a soul's journey over the course of many lives to learn how to create justice, fairness, harmony, and peace. It isn't about knowing these things already, which is a common misperception about Libra. Someone with this placement has many lives of trying to figure out the right way to go about creating those states. When humans are trying to learn something they often veer to one extreme of its expression and sometimes then back to the other extreme. This is especially true of Pluto placements because we are trying to dig deep into the unconscious to find out what it will take to be powerful in a given situation. In my case I have other lives associated with my soul on the timeline that are honestly and legitimately exploring if violence is justifiable when I am annoyed and pained to the point of living a low quality of life and being limited in or prevented in doing work I know is of benefit to others. In this particular instance in a situation in which for me to accomplish what I happen to believe is a fantastically awesome, stupendously rad greater good (creating the work that I do) I might have to do something drastic to have the necessary peace and quiet.

Think about people you know with Pluto in Libra, those born between 1971-2 and 1984. They will not most of them own any such thoughts or feelings but in them these emotions and ideas are present even if only deep under the surface. They are hidden because what goes hand in hand with exploring ways to create peace, harmony, justice, etc., is judgment and aversion to being unkind or, taken further, violent. Pluto ruled by Venus wants to be and be taken as loving, generous, gentle, and good but Pluto is Pluto: It represents the portions of consciousness that we want to label ugly and banish from our minds and hearts. But we can never do so. It exists under the surface in each person until it is dealt with, in the mean time forming shadows parts we do not own and are afraid to experience. In Libra, being unfair and stepping on others is a large chunk of the shadow terrain. Doing what it takes to get what one wants is part of this. People in this astrological generation are likely to carry fears about acting in their own self-interest to the point of possibly infringing upon others. Those you know with this signature will believe that they are kind, etc., and some of them will have issues owning their assertiveness because of fears of being aggressive. Remember that Pluto leads us now and then to explore extreme behavior and you will see that avoiding self-assertion to attempt to avoid being selfish or cruel is just as much a mistake as taking what one wants at all costs even if it hurts others.

In the end I'm not willing to do anything like this (kill dogs) in this life but I do have to deal with the emotional realities and input of these other manifestations of my soul located at other points along the Earth timeline. If I don't then I am just reliving those other lives through repression and occasional explosion and I have to tell you that that seems pretty unimaginative to me. If there's anything I know about those other lives of ours situated along the time-space continuum it's that we often make choices and do things without all the facts. It's part of the learning curve of the human trip. Doing this kind of astrology we can know that we are missing some of the facts and make adjustments accordingly. I'm in possession of certain perspectives in this life that prevent me from being willing to do things half-considered and half-baked.

There is a feeling that comes with such parts of self or manifestations of soul worth mentioning. It is the sense of knee-jerk necessity and a cessation of reasoned thought and considered feeling that feels skewed or incomplete. Whenever something in me is reactive and I can't see through it to know clearly what kind of response I might like to generate to a given situation, I can pretty much bet that there is a thing in play relating to another life in which that manifestation of my soul doesn't have the same insights and experiences that I do. If I give in to the impulse to react in a certain way I usually feel like I'm being used, actually. Just about every time in the end I regret it so I've learned to check my reactions as best I can. It's interesting to view my life as a series of experiences of the moment and simultaneously a set of triggers from my soul's other manifestations along the Earth timeline. It certainly alters and modifies (and perhaps upgrades) what I think a human is!

Now the weather is not as hot as when the dog barking was such an issue. It's winter and even winter in Tucson has some cold-like attributes. The dogs are less inspired to bark all the time and I suspect they are not left out as often or as long on a daily basis by their humans. This part of me still exists and makes his opinion known – he is ready to procure materials and execute his violent peace-creating plan at a moment's notice – and still I proceed with my life as I choose. During the few months when all of this came to a head I did work less and sort of throw my arms up in the air in protest numerous times. I was on a roll with producing videos and had to cease because of the noise and stress. The energetic cost of trying to work through and around that level and frequency of angry and anger-inducing noise was too high and I lost some of my willingness to churn out book after book and MP3 after MP3. I still love offering to others what I am able to offer but there are times when circumstance just isn't conducive to getting things done. At the time of this writing J. and I are preparing to move and there will be extra scrutiny about the noise level in the neighborhood before we make a commitment to a new place.

A Naïve Outlaw

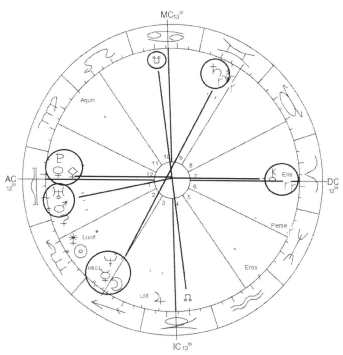

Covered in this chapter: Pluto-Venus-Pallas Athene in Libra with Venus-Pallas square the nodes, Mars-Uranus in the 1st square the nodes, Chiron-Eris in Aries/7th square the nodes, SN ruler Moon conjunct Neptune and opposing Saturn, SN in the 10th.

At one point when living in LA I realized that I was checking out the guns on all the cops I'd see around the city. One part of me insisted it was strange that people carry guns and that seemed to be the issue but another part of me was nervous when seeing the weapons out in the open. This went on for months but I didn't catch on to the idea that there was something under the surface that needed to be dealt with. I was also in general nervous being anywhere near police or anyone with guns including a time at LAX when I walked past Army dudes with combat rifles in the midst of some jacked-up terror alert.

Is it inevitable that living in LA yields parking tickets and/or moving violations? With the energy on the streets and highways I wonder about this. I found myself doing an illegal U-turn when picking up my girlfriend A. from work one night. I was having a particularly stressful night due to what I would call Mercury-Neptune and 12th-house issues which are really control issues. I was missing turns and forgetting things and was late to pick her up. No matter what I did I just couldn't get my head on straight. By the time I got to West LA I was just about a raving lunatic. I did the U-turn and a police cruiser pulled me over.

In that stressed state I was not my normal self – far from it. In interacting with the officers I realized they thought I was on a substance or five. I stepped back and looked at myself and my energy and to me it looked like I might have been on PCP! Let's just say that this was a time when stress and constant forgetfulness and bumbling would affect me much more than today. Before getting deeply grounded (a.k.a. *sane*) I used to be so entirely frustrated with these material-world clusterexpletives that I would feel that I was losing my mind. Objects and tools wouldn't work IF I could find them – and this was just about the apex of that sort of experience.

So I got this moving violation and then went to get A. about a block away. She was worried and I told her what had happened and that I needed her to drive us home. We got there fine and I collapsed, happy to put the experience behind me.

I became afraid to deal with the citation and in time let the deadline for doing so in an easy fashion pass. It wasn't long before I was feeling entirely irrational about it and avoiding it. Then one day months later I received a letter from some local governmental office outlining the penalties and fines now tacked on to the original citation. I almost panicked! It was something like triple the original amount. Don't ask what I was thinking all the months prior to that – I was trying not to think of it at all.

A. pulled me aside after I'd opened the letter and looked me in the eyes and told me she loved me and she would help me figure this out. I felt on the verge of losing my sanity and I could tell it was deep fear coming to the surface. She helped me calm down and her support was so needed! I felt at the time that I could not have faced the reality of that letter and done anything mature about it without that support.

I called to make arrangements to go to court and face the music. As the date approached I dreaded going. It is no exaggeration to say that I was terrified. I became aware of a part of me that feared the thought of police and judges and the justice and legal systems. During this period the volume on noticing guns on police officers was cranked up and I would be downright scared when I saw one, eying them cautiously and practically walking on eggshells around them. After the court date – when everything went well as I stood up in front of a judge and plead guilty to the moving violation and took the disapproving look and paid the money – I called a friend at the time with whom I would trade sessions. She does intuitive work, energy reading, and reads other-life issues as well as brings in disembodied helpers such as angels and ascended masters. She saw a life in which I am a generally harmless young man in the American West in the 19th century who gets involved with the wrong people. At first pranks are pulled and then someone in the group decides it would be a good idea to rob a bank and they do that a few times. It seems pretty harmless and no one ever gets hurt … until someone does. In one robbery a bystander is killed and this young man sort of wakes up and realizes that things are a bit out of control. He sees that he had not been paying attention and let himself get into the wrong stuff with the wrong people. The gang splits up to go into hiding and he goes off on his own, determined never to do anything criminal again and living in constant fear of being caught. My friend told me laughingly that no one was coming to get me and I finally saw what she was seeing, able to apply some context to the feelings I'd been having that were making me so afraid.

Pluto in Libra journeys in part have to do with dealing with the effects on others of our choices. *Sure, go ahead and do what you want* ... and then realize that your actions affect others. Mars-Uranus in Libra/1st square the nodes in part relates to doing what you want and at least for a time being irrelevant whether through choice or neglect failing to notice that you affect others. I feel each of these energies strongly in this young man who simply isn't interested in paying attention to what he's doing and the ramifications his choices might have.

Having the SN in the 10th house describes being known by the community for something. Oftentimes one becomes known for what he or she does for a living or how one functions in the public sphere. Fame is one possibility and infamy is another and, as it happens, over the course of many lives each will be experienced by those with 10th house SNs. Below I will describe elements of a life as a writer who was well known for doing something positive but this chapter is about the infamy that can come from life in the 10th house. Perhaps there were wanted posters with this man's name and face on them and perhaps it was just that his name was known as a criminal. Either way he didn't feel safe and he was sure the authorities were out to get him.

Also in this thread of consciousness I see the naïveté possible when the SN ruler conjuncts Neptune. This signature can lead one to be Neptunian – including ungrounded, escapist, unaware, and not in touch with reality – to the point that all sorts of things unfold seemingly of their own free will and apparently without one's conscious involvement. All the energies in our charts are present in our energy fields and psyches but we don't have to use all of them. Those that we do not actively use still draw life experiences to us that seem to force us to choose reactions to them. In other words, just because we don't make a conscious choice in some part of life doesn't mean that a choice will not be made. For this naïve outlaw, letting the situation get out of hand was less through straight-up stupidity (as it may appear to outside observers) than through failing to make an active choice one way or the other.

With Venus in Libra/12th and Chiron-Eris in Aries/7th in opposition and square the nodal axis, there is also an issue at times with saying "yes" and "no" to the appropriate people at the appropriate times. The signature indicates that boundaries, making choices of playmates, and working on relationship dynamics that don't work can trigger considerable confusion in me at times. Chiron-Eris in Aries/7th can indicate that the chart holder can become afraid to tell others what he wants or needs or to tell others "no" to what they want and need. A result can be getting swept away in the currents of what other people feel like doing. In this life the consequences are more akin to seeing movies my friends and girlfriends have wanted to see and eating in annoying French restaurants, cafes, and bistros instead of anything I might prefer – not a big deal at all! But in other lives this kind of thing can be more extreme.

I sense that this young man has some pretty good radar for what the right kinds of situations are for him but that he never learns to trust it, giving the reins too much of the time to others with whom he is involved while not being picky about who they are. He seems to feel that his preferences don't matter all that much. If you don't get that you're in charge of your life you might defer to the decisions and wills of others with the worst-case scenario being something like what happens with this young man. If you surrender your will to others and haven't checked them out, you might just find yourself getting into trouble and not being sure how to get out of it.

The fear that was triggered in LA by seeing police personnel sporting guns was that they were or would be coming for me. It was a few months until I could hear sirens or see flashing cop lights and not be on edge and a couple of years before I was comfortable standing or walking near someone with a gun on his or her hip. I did a series of affirmations to forgive myself across time for anything I might have done that was wrong or that hurt others. Now when I do affirmations I'm able to fine-tune them and identify the exact emotional trigger and so choose the right words easily but then I sort of fumbled around with the ideas as affirmations. It really was a fake-it-til-you-make-it kind of thing, which is why it took so long to make real progress.

This happened around early 2007. A couple of years later I was able to own the fact that other mes living lives on different points along the Earth timeline are making choices that don't feel that great and of which I might feel the reverberation now. Whether there is some egregious crime or something minor involved I learned that it is the perception of doing wrong that can imprint an energy body karmically that will affect the other human lives elsewhere on the timeline. If I feel guilty about forgetting to feed my cat once or twice I can create a knot in my field that may grow and combine with other things to feed a story about how I am irresponsible or can't do things right (or anything else this could seem to mean for a person) and failing to feed a cat once in a while is certainly not a crime. I was able to make peace with the perspective offered by Ascended Master Djehuty that each of us is trying to learn what love is, where it comes from, and who is responsible for giving it to whom and that along the way we are each at times making some pretty bone-headed moves in that direction. No one is free from actions, behaviors, and choices that seem or are wrong or destructive but at some point we each must forgive ourselves if we are to advance as beings. We need to take responsibility for what we do and have done yet also introduce a measure of compassion that reflects what the wrong and wrong-seeming experiences are have been about from the soul's vantage point: learning about what it means, requires, and costs to live human lives.

At this point on my path to learn about love I am able to recognize that I am the being who does all these things in all the lives. I am able to accept it and I am willing to have compassion for myself as a being fumbling through life while usually forgetting my true nature as a Divine creator. I am in fact remembering slowly. Owning up to all these memories bleeding through from across the Earth timeline is a first step in owning my power as a creative being. I can't be present now if I don't accept and make peace with all aspects of my self including those that do things that might not be that great for self and other. I accept that I am in the process of remembering how to be the source of love and I am fine with owning that many different kinds of experiences have been the vehicles for this education.

Blame, shame, and guilt are the greatest impediments to spiritual evolution. Learning about love is the name of game when it comes to growth as energetic, conscious beings. Negative views of others reflect negative views of ourselves. Such views keep us from exploring the process of letting go of meaning ascribed to the past so that we may become present to who we are in this moment. We can choose to let go of identities formed in the past as a result of our human experiences and consider all that has happened to us as necessary raw material for the learning journey of souls embodied as humans.

So, each of us does various kinds of things at some points along these long and complex journeys to learn about what love is, where it comes from, and who is responsible for giving it to whom. Are we each willing to reframe what it all means? Are we each willing to accept what we've created and move on?

Regarding this naïve outlaw, I feel him in me from time to time. I no longer feel the same kind of nervous or worry when I see someone carrying a gun but I do notice them, and in general this part (and perhaps other parts) of me get a bit nervous. Recently in a local grocery store I saw a man in a cowboy hat and boots to match with a six shooter in a gun belt on his hip. I kept staring at him because he was not in any sort of uniform. I realized then that I also pause occasionally at the doors of businesses here in Tucson because many have notices on the front doors and windows that no weapons are allowed. It's not still the Old West here but apparently there's a bit of a hangover from those times. But I no longer fear that anyone's coming to get me because I did something wrong and this is progress.

I can see the dissonance in me about guns in general and recently considered taking a gun education class. This would include learning to shoot a hand gun. I did research on local options and imagined that if I knew how to handle one the mystery might be dissolved and along with it the remnant of the fear of guns. I may end up taking such a class but for now I'm staying in the space of letting these parts talk to me. The other parts that might be associated with this gun issue could be soldiers from different parts of the timeline. I know I have that sort of history as well and have loved and hated it and, at times, I did not feel ready to undertake that path but did it anyway. I have an almost seismic emotional response to the song "Over There" by

George M. Cohan.   My heart opens and suddenly everything is very serious, deep, and intense. That song is from World War I, for the record. I haven't been able to dig down deep enough to get to know that other-life karmic part of my soul even after watching the movie "Yankee Doodle Dandy," Cohan's life story. The movie ends with the beginning of the USA's entrance to WWI. Just like when I was a kid and watched that movie a number of times my heart strings were fully and robustly strummed when that tune was played and sung.

A Seeker or Two

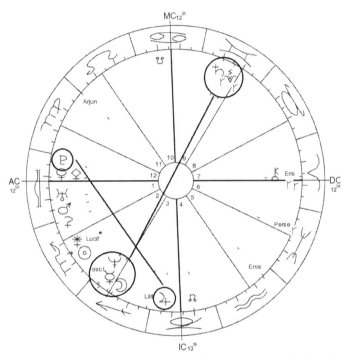

Covered in this chapter: Pluto in the 12th square Jupiter in Capricorn/3rd, SN ruler Moon in Sagittarius conjunct true Black Moon Lilith-Neptune-Mercury.

When we met A. had been regularly attending a breathing class taught by a Tantra teacher near where I lived. It was the first activity she suggested doing together so after talking for the first time we met at the teacher's house and I experienced my first class. I loved it and over the next 6 months or so I attended most Sunday evenings.

Each Sunday class was basically the same. There was a series of breaths that were taught more or less in an order but one Sunday he taught a different set of breaths. He said they had been taught in the West infrequently and I surmised that the techniques were considered powerful. We've all heard about Eastern people guarding their powerful teachings and keeping them secret from outsiders who might misunderstand and misuse them, right? This was to be filed under that heading.

When the teacher began explaining and demonstrating the set a part of me came forward and was absolutely rapt. I was more focused than I'd been on anything in a long time – perhaps more so than on anything at any other time in my life. The part of me that was observing, the grounded and centered part, was watching this and knew something interesting was coming to light. The part of me that came forward felt that *finally* I was gaining secret knowledge that I'd always wanted. During the class that night I did three things simultaneously: learned the techniques/participated in the class, experienced what that part was thinking and feeling, and observed and tried to learn about this part of me.

I don't know and it doesn't matter if these particular techniques are in this seeker's awareness in his life. This is one life on which I don't have much detail, only the feeling of insatiable curiosity for Eastern secret knowledge. I suspect that any breathing techniques actually or purported to be from the Orient (his word) would have had this man sitting up in his seat.

About him I sense a life of mind and study, perhaps of being or playing at being an academic whether in a formal setting or not. I don't get a religious vibe from him at all but a focus on reaching out to learn new things. I have the feeling that he would regularly and periodically exhaust everyone around him with questions on his mind that no one he knew could answer. He feels to be in/from the 19th century but this is one of those things I can't explain beyond my sense of it especially given the impressions I've gotten from spirits of the dead while working as a medium and extensive work with parts of people alive on other portions of the Earth timeline. He feels Northern European to me and he wants to know everything.

Pluto in the 12th house indicates a deep need and drive to understand life itself. Sometimes I've felt into this other-life persona and he indicates that he needs to know the secrets of the cosmos. Living in Western culture has made many people over time intensely curious about those other people, those in the East who have such different philosophies, religions, and ways of living. Pluto in the 12th doesn't directly implicate a philosophical or religious search but this planet here can symbolize an insatiable curiosity, even a lust for mystical or spiritual experience. The square to Jupiter in Capricorn/3rd in this context can represent philosophical and religious ideas or education that inspire, pressure, or drive the need for understanding into the terrain of "insatiable." Jupiter squaring this Pluto might make the 12th-house quest a bit of an obsession as each new thing learned has the potential to deepen the hunger for new information. In some contexts this square can indicate that Jupiterian others bring pressure to my 12th-house mission through friction and/or criticism yet here I get the sense that the learning itself is what drove this man, not conflicts or misunderstandings with Jupiterian others. Perhaps there are Jupiterian figures in his life on that other portion of the timeline who interfere with his quest for ultimate truth but memories of such people don't come through when I tune into his thoughts and feelings.

The SN ruler in Sagittarius and its conjunctions and oppositions also contribute to this story. Any SN ruler in Sagittarius indicates that the person shows up in many lives as one kind of seeker or another. Many human karmic stories involving Sagittarius point to dabbling in, exploring, doubting, questioning, trying on for size, or diving head-first into religion in one form or another. Religions have been central to humanity's search for truth for a long time and even though we might think of religion in terms of the big three monotheistic religions, as long as there have been humans here there's been some form of religion in which we have been dabbling. In the 3rd house and conjunct Mercury, this SN ruler describes a human who is a student, teacher, writer, and thinker. Definitely someone who is curious in a fundamentally deep way and highly likely someone who has something to say. The conjunction to Neptune underscores Pluto in the 12th as it brings mysticism and other Neptunian ways of being into the mix. Neptune here can bring a lack of boundaries and borders when it comes to learning, teaching, and speaking. The true Black moon Lilith is here, as well. It adds the flavors instinctive, visceral, lower-chakra, and earthy to the stellium and indicates that the learning and communication of this person can be erratic and cover much ground. The combination of Lilith, Neptune, and Mercury in Sagittarius conjunct the 3rd-house SN ruler can inspire a person to be rather ungrounded and unfocused or perhaps deeply focused but not always thinking clearly. The imagination and curiosity can be out of proportion to everything else and, in fact, consuming.

Now, I have at times in this life seemed and felt as though I want to know everything. When I was younger it was most certainly true and then a decade ago when I was ushered (read *tossed*) head-first onto my very own slippy-slidey spiritual path I found that the symbolic language that is astrology helps me answer what I in fact had always wanted to know but had not previously isolated: why people think, believe, and do what they think, believe, and do. The various topics I'd explored in sometimes rapid-fire associative mode for years took a back seat to learning all I could about that single metaphysical language perspective. When I lived in the Boston area I would be at the huge public library almost weekly "following up on leads" – things that had sparked my curiosity whether met through dialogue, media, or – most often – something that had come before. There were chains of leads that took me in a number of different directions that had me reading, researching, and going to lectures, talks, films, panels, performances, and museums for a lot of my 6½ years there.

The opposition from Saturn-Vesta in Gemini/9th to the SN ruler can manifest situations in which authority figures (Saturn) dedicated (Vesta) to learning and teaching (Gemini) can oppose my curiosity and need to gather knowledge. I will say that in this life the people who are least important to me are those who can but refuse to answer questions. When younger, in school at times when I had questions that weren't deemed appropriate for the unfolding trajectory of the lesson plan and asked them of reluctant teachers, I quickly found out who I could respect and who was (the feeling went) not worth my time. I had already gone through "orientation" with this at home: after years of asking my mom all kinds of questions about many different things she began directing me to "look it up in the World Book," our encyclopedia. In principle it was fine but when I couldn't interact with others and dialogue with questions and answers it was a bit of a let down. Understanding doesn't come from facts for me but from the chemistry and associations within my mind possible through interaction – the Sagittarius stellium sextiles Pluto-Venus in Libra/12th and trines Chiron in Aries/7th. In short, others are preferred over books. As it happens I have many memories of resorting to the World Book to learn a fact or two and being bummed about it. The phrase, "look it up in the World Book" was repeated so often by my mom that it became truncated to "look it up" and it clanged and banged around in my head for years afterward.

In truth it made me a bit hesitant to ask others my questions. Now I can see that in terms of the energy matrix in my chart, I needed to be driven to learn things my own way when and how I wanted to learn them. With Saturn-Vesta in Gemini/9th opposing SN ruler in Sagittarius/3rd there is no question that there are lives on the Earth timeline during which various mes are tearing their hair out because they can't get the answers they seek. The opposition tells the story of someone seeking knowledge and finding road blocks from and in the form of others who are guarding information or how it is used and spread. No wonder this part came to the surface in that breath class! *Finally* the secrets were being revealed.

But Neptune in the mix with the SN ruler also speaks of a desire to alter consciousness. This can be done in many ways of course but I have had a fear and dread of altering my consciousness in particular through chemical means and it makes me sit up and notice the part carrying it. I shied away from everything chemical but alcohol for years. I'm sure I did and now do seem like a stick in the mud, prude, sheltered, and/or naïve. About 4 or 5 years ago I felt into it when watching a movie featuring the use of injected recreational drugs. Always had I cringed and then started covering my eyes when needles in movies were at hand. Really I just couldn't stand it. When I felt into it I realized that it was sourced in some life in which some me does use drugs and probably of various kinds but those injected seem to trigger me the most. Watching the characters prepare their treats just about did me in! In time I was avoiding movies that I knew contained depictions of drug use.

I came to connect with a feeling that I had messed myself up in some other life doing drugs. I'd already had the sense that I never wanted to lose control of my consciousness but that is general and likely related to a number of different experiences in various lives that relate to me having Pluto in the 12th house sextile Neptune in Sagittarius – there is bound to be some wide-ranging consciousness stretching and manipulation in the spirit of expansion but things don't always go well when you mess around with what belongs in the 12th house. This thing with the injected drugs is specific and when I tune into its frequency I'm able to feel that the dread and fear in fact cover over sadness, regret, pain from loss, and a generalized sense of letting myself down and ending up a miserable failure.

I don't know if the part mentioned in the first part of this chapter is a person who injected himself with drugs in his search for expanded consciousness and secret knowledge. If not, the insatiable curiosity he feels not for mere information and knowledge but wisdom does in fact resonate with a person – another life's me – who might explore chemical alteration in that spirit of the search for truth and meaning. It's clear to me at this point that what I've experienced in getting to the place from which I can do mediumship, work with my and others' spirit guides, and channel an ascended master reflects a long-term and progressive alteration of consciousness. I refer to my path to get here as one riddled with "software" or consciousness upgrades, as I had to have my perceptual and processing faculties worked on by guides and masters to open me to be able to bring through their messages for others. And so I definitely live with an altered consciousness that results from my seeking secret knowledge! Working with Ascended Master Djehuty began when I asked (sort of tongue-in-cheekly) if there were any benevolent beings floating around who might be interested in helping me understand the nature and multilife journey of soul that I wasn't finding in religious, spiritual, or metaphysical/astrological literature and minds. I asked some interesting questions I hadn't heard others ask and from him I began to get answers that rang true.

These days I do have some issues with tracking the passage and unfolding of time, another Neptunian issue that reflects at least some level of altered consciousness. I don't lose my keys, wallet, and glasses but if I didn't live with someone who has a regular office job or have clients scheduled at particular times I suspect I'd get lost in each week. Today I realized that I told a client I'd record her MP3 reading for her and mail the CD within a week and that was 6 days ago. I experience that conversation in my memory as a day or two ago.

Most of my life I've been unable to follow recipes because I forget the ingredient listed, the volume of it to use, and/or what I'm supposed to do with it as soon as my eyes leave the page. It's actually comical and is fine as long as I don't want anything that needs to use a recipe! But the last few years it has extended to forgetting all manner of things even if they are written down and even if I am looking at them. Triple-checking client data is my norm.

The point here is that in this life I most definitely live through an altered state of consciousness that extends beyond simple, occasional forgetfulness. Since my Pluto is in the 12th sextile the Sagittarius stellium involving Neptune – indicating that I need to alter my consciousness in some way (ideally for the better!) – it has come to unfold anyway.

This brings up an interesting point regarding the notion of changing karma explored in the introduction. I teach that there is no such thing as destiny but that there are themes set out by your soul – the portion of cosmic consciousness that is you – that cannot be avoided. With awareness you can many times change the parameters and make choices about how it happens but the thing that your soul sets out for you will happen. In my case related to this example, I was going to have to figure out a way to live in the 12th house with Pluto sextile Neptune and I most certainly could have chosen drugs, but it didn't feel right to me. It inspired fear because of experiences elsewhere on the timeline and I knew I could choose to do something differently. In the end I was not doing it and so it came to me in the form of an intuitive or psychic opening a decade ago, but I did have free will about how to respond to and approach it. It was just about as frightening as I imagine getting lost with drug use/abuse/addiction would be but in the end it's been empowering for me to learn to live in multiple worlds at the same time. Bridging multiple worlds in some ways is a positive expression of living in the 12th house if the route experienced is about consciousness and awareness. To stay grounded in the body and anchor something of other dimensions or planes in this one is what I spend a lot of time doing. I feel very fortunate to have learned in this life what I have and it pleases me greatly to teach and counsel about living a Neptunian life that isn't centered on and doesn't stop with, "Well, no one understands it and you just kinda get swept away by stuff outside your control and your toilet might leak/basement might flood," and the like, a stereotype I seem to have when it comes to commonplace astrological approaches to Neptune based in an unwillingness to understand what it is truly about.

A Writer

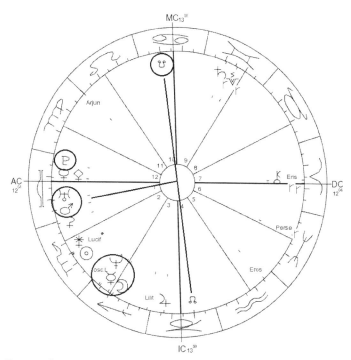

MC 13⁵⁰

Arjun

AC 12ˢᵗ

DC 12⁰⁴

Eris

Perse

Lucif

osc L

Eros

Lilit

IC 13⁵⁹

Covered in this chapter: Pluto in Libra, SN in the 10ᵗʰ house, Uranus in Libra square the nodes, SN ruler Moon in Sagittarius conjunct Neptune-Mercury.

This story has been central to my life for a number of reasons. It is the one of the group included here on which I have the individual's biographical and birth data though I do not share it with others. In time I might but for now I'll work with the themes in play in his life that have helped me heal issues in this life.

When I was in my 20s I finally admitted to myself that I felt that I was a writer while acknowledging that I didn't have a subject. It was a strange place to be in for most of my life – knowing something about me is true but having little to no experience or confidence to do it. There was nothing that made me sit down and work with words outside some play with friends in college, wherein we created a series of characters and each wrote silly stories involving them.

I did plenty of writing in the process of school work including a thesis required for graduation at my college. But I didn't know what *I* had to say. After moving from small-town Ohio to Boston I met a woman who told me with certainty that I am a writer and encouraged me to explore that side of myself. With her I began a process of playing with words but then the floodgates opened and I was doing it on my own, without her prodding. There was one moment in which I was resistant to writing, she said something intended to help me flow with the words, and then everything changed and I almost couldn't stop. The shift was triggered by her suggestion that we play a writing game like the Dadaists and Surrealists in which one person writes a sentence and the other person adds the next and the paper is handed back and forth until something seems to have taken shape, even if nonsensical. I paused when she gave me the paper with her first sentence on it and she noticed this, asking me what was wrong. I told her I didn't

132

know what to write next. She said, "Write what comes next," and the floodgate opened. Suddenly I saw what to do and imagination was flowing. At that point I was set to begin a graduate certificate in trombone performance at a conservatory in Boston a few weeks later. I began writing and was unable to pick up the horn to practice, making music performance out of the question. I deferred and ended up not beginning the program. I was so enamored with the feeling of words flowing out that I didn't touch the horn in a full year, unthinkable to who I had been since I was 10 years old.

But that's just an anecdote to comment on the importance of writing in my life. The point is that it was not always a welcome activity and then suddenly it was and, in fact, consumed me. Before this I had doubted that anything I might write would be good and sure that no one would want to read it. Some of this is general Pluto-in-Libra stuff about fearing the other won't or can't hear you or that others are unavailable to share experience with you. As I look back on it the idea that my writing wouldn't be good enough seems to be a bit silly given what I know now about my natural writing process: get as much out on paper as wants to get out and then edit and delete later. My Sagittarian mind does best when allowed to flow and improvise.

The full story on my learning about, opening to, and integrating the bleed-through of this writer is a bit too long for the scope of this work and, as mentioned above, there are details I don't share. I do perceive that some of those details would allow the story to be fleshed out (what a tease I am, right?). Suffice it to say that I was aware of this writer's work and deeply affected from my first exposure to it. I intuited much about his thought process before I had his chart and began having emotional and sense memories that I now understand belong to him on his part of the timeline. When doing work on him in college a professor familiar with it remarked to me that he didn't know where I was getting my information but that it was great work. Even reading biographical and interpretive material on the writer's life and work I had a visceral sense of agreement with some points and clarity that others were misguided or incorrect. When I wrote a paper on him in college (long before I had a sense that this could be another life of my soul) I knew with absolute certainty that what I had been taught in classes about his ideas was not the full picture and, actually, missed key points central to what he was saying. After an epiphanic moment while working on that paper I presented what I felt sure he had meant that had been misunderstood by a number of readers and teachers and this is what garnered the praise from my teacher. The central approach to his work accepted in academic circles is based on this misunderstanding, in fact, and I had gained insights from within my own energy field to see through it.

At one point several years later I had a strong intuitive hit to try on for size the notion that my "insider" knowledge of him was more than coincidence. I had seen his chart and wondered at its similarities with mine. I told the story to a friend I knew could be objective about it and she said it seemed that I had picked up where he left off but was going to do the writing thing differently. I knew that introducing spiritual perspectives was part of that as he wrote from his mind almost exclusively.

One thing to note about this man is that he was well-received both with fiction and non-fiction and won some awards for his work. When the few people here and there who know about my creative work in this life rave about it to me (I'm not tooting my own horn, I promise!) this part of me is not surprised. I attribute this to the expectation of accolades this writer on another part of the timeline is experiencing. He has a solid confidence in his literary self and expression and I've allowed that to creep into and to some degree blossom in my life. My South Node in the 10th house represents not just being well-known in some lives but also now and then having done something or things that are praised by a community. Life in the 10th house when it can be categorized as anything other than infamy involves achievement and accomplishment while being recognized for it. Our stories of ambition and work ethic play themselves out in this house and this writer – at least as an adult, how I sense him – had no doubts about his talents and the worth of what he had to say. Routinely I hear from clients who sense that it is important that they write a book something like, "But who would want to read it? What about me is so special?" A few years ago I might have related to them but having integrated this other-life persona I feel assured that if a person believes in what he or she has to say then it is worth saying and worth sharing with others.

Working on and publishing the first three nonfiction books was a bit nerve-wracking even as I felt I had to do it. *Living Myth* and *Seeing Through Spiritual Eyes* were somewhat challenging but each was short and didn't present a vision or a teaching that had to be organized and laid out in just the right way. The former is comprised of a number of chapters each on a mythological figure. Each is a view into an archetypal process that we live in our day-to-day lives and as such each chapter can stand alone as a short work. In the latter I describe my personal 7-year process of opening to intuition and working with spirit guides, the spirits of the dead, and ascended masters. It is a personal account of what I experienced and learned and, again, didn't present a single teaching I had to methodically plan and execute. *The Soul's Journey I: Astrology, Reincarnation, and Karma with a Medium and Channel* caused the most stress because I felt I was making my first statement in writing that I believe myself to be an astrologer with something valuable to say. To complete that book I had to begin believing that I have the right to be heard and others would want to read it. This writer from another part of the timeline seems always to have believed this about himself and I had to come to believe it, too. With Pluto in Libra I had a part of me doubting that others would want to hear it because there have been times in my life when it seemed that no one on the planet was available to me for much of anything. I understand now that that kind of loneliness represents echoes of what is happening on other parts of the timeline but at those times, living through them, this was not at all clear.

Another thread from the writer's life that I feel strongly within me is to do with when loved ones use recreational substances to the point of damaging behavior to themselves. In a chapter above I noted my personal issue about losing my self and mind through drug use in another life but this man didn't do that. He instead lost connection to women he loved (including one he married) to that way of living. I feel acutely the pain when someone I'm involved with borders on destructive or damaging choices when it comes to substances of any kind whether recreational or medicinal. I feel them as absent and it almost feels like I'm losing them, bordering on a fear of losing them to death. The writer was at times unable to get through to some women he loved and I feel this as pain and a frankly desperate need to connect with full presence with women I love. In earlier years I wasn't very present myself and so this is really about relationships in the last decade or so of my life. For many reasons I was for years not grounded, in my body, or happy about being alive. The process I've gone through to learn to be a medium and channel and do the metaphysical work that I do has turned that around and I find myself often craving unmediated, undiluted, conscious contact with the woman with whom I'm involved.

Another thread from this man's life that I deal with now has to do with cheating on those women he loved.

I've always had very strong opinions about fidelity and while once in college I found myself strongly attracted to a woman other than my partner at the time, I haven't cheated on anyone. Some women I've been with have explored other options without communicating to me that they are doing it (I'm looking for a better way to describe it than "cheating" – I see that I'm triggered into judgment by that word). As one person I've confided in about this life story who's done research on the writer said, the writer seems to have had a woman in every port. This isn't to be taken literally but he wasn't faithful all the time and perhaps he was faithful to no one. Now I find myself in a relationship in which my needs and desires are not always met; my partner is often unavailable to play with me in the ways that I want and need. She was the first to bring up the idea of an open relationship so that I could be happy but at the time I resisted it. I came around after over a year of stress from trying to figure out better ways to give her space to take care of her own stuff so that she could be more present with me and better ways to approach her so that we can play together in ways that work well for each of us. Many times it seems to me that this relationship is in my life in part to force me to begin looking outside it to meet my needs but in an open way that would heal other life stories of infidelity. For years my guides have suggested to me that eventually I'll find it important to have open relationships in which I might have multiple partners but there will be no secrets or subterfuge. I'm still in the process of adjusting to the idea and have been discussing it with some friends and family yet I don't now know what will be best way for me to be in relationship.

My Pluto-in-Libra preference is to put my attention on one woman but my Uranus-in-Libra learning (including that it is in the 1st house and square the nodal axis) seems to include retaining independence in relationship and not putting all my attention on one woman. My partner at present is a wonderful person with whom to have these discussions not only because she's researched and explored polyamory but also because we share a level of communication that is the deepest and strongest I've experienced with anyone in this life. She also gets that the human journey has in large part to do with learning about what love is, where it comes from, and who is responsible for giving it to whom. Her own Uranus in Libra square her Ascendant-Descendant axis has brought her to experiences that have taught her much about the realities of relationships among people working toward spiritual growth while cleaning up the emotional past from this life and others. She seems to have learned that at times one other person cannot be the be-all, end-all for another who is learning, changing, healing, and growing.

Finally, the last thread to share of the writer's life that bleeds through and that I've had to learn to integrate is that he was focused on this world and this life. He believed this was the only life you get and he was therefore oriented toward material reality. He spent his life also more or less going back and forth between his mind and his body. I have the same tendency to leave out spirit and

139

the energetic side of life but have had to learn to adjust. His writing most of his life was intellectual and he didn't share anything personal in it or allow his heart and emotional self to be present in his work. At every turn over the last decade I've been nudged to do that and I have, though at times it has been work to overcome the standards for writing and what it means to be a professional that my mind has put in place and upon which it insists. This bleed-through part feels that being in the mind is the only way to go and that everything else is nonsense.

The book that you are reading is proof of those changes but it's also in the work I do with my clients and students. I routinely share not just personal stories with them but also insights into my emotional and energetic reactions to astrological events and life situations. Astrology is a symbolic language of life and if I were solely in my mind – which is a habit and indeed knee-jerk preference – then I couldn't present work that affects people deeply in positive ways. This book would not exist had I not integrated what this writer has to say but firmly committed to making my own decisions that serve my evolution. This life as Tom Jacobs is a chance to be in the heart in a new way and an opportunity (important though challenging) to bring my feeling side and human sensitivity into my work and writing. It is a regular occurrence that I receive heart-felt thanks for something I've written or produced and it feels good to include heart as well as to see the results. For years I was hesitant to do it because I tend to default to rather private (I'm a Scorpio with Venus conjunct Pluto in the 12th house, after all!) but in a great many situations I intuitively sense that the explanation that would make sense to the person with whom I am speaking is a story from my own life. And here you are reading a book of stories from my own life! Parts of me aren't sure if I should be embarrassed but other parts of me are sure it's good to reveal this information about myself in the spirit of helping others understand more about soul and its multilife human trip.

A Man Who Loses Everything

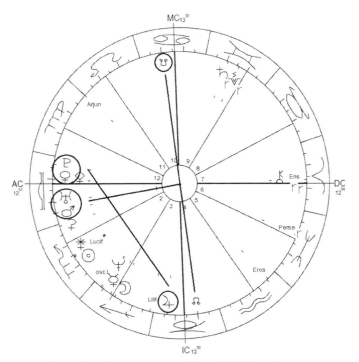

Covered in this chapter: SN in the 10th, Pluto-Venus in Libra/12th, Pluto square Jupiter in Capricorn/3rd, Mars-Uranus in Libra/1st square the nodes.

In the Spring of 2008 at a meeting of Steve Forrest's Apprenticeship Program my name came of the "sorting hat" to have my chart used as an example of the topics featured during the workshop. Steve sometimes presents introductory material on the chosen workshop theme for a day or two and then uses a handful of students' charts to bring the principles to life on the following days. The theme of this workshop was intentionally approaching transits and progressions. The person whose name was drawn could choose what themes on which Steve would focus in the mini-reading. I was coming up on transiting Pluto square natal Pluto and I had been thinking about the potentials in terms of my natal Pluto-Venus conjunction in the 12th house square Jupiter. Choosing to have faith in life or anything good has at times been an issue my life and I knew that one interpretation of a square from Pluto in the 12th house to Jupiter could be a huge risk taken at some point in some life that doesn't pan out. It is a signature that can leave a person irrationally exuberant, bereft of all hope, or manically swinging back and forth between the two.

To begin the story Steve set things up by looking at my South Node in the 10th house in Cancer, a marker of someone who can be a devoted servant and leader to his community. He painted a picture of me as a nurturing figure to my community in some life, perhaps a native community on the North American continent hundreds of years ago. Through tying in other symbols he created a story of the community being overwhelmed by a technologically superior force. With my 10th-house South Node he said it was safe to assume that I was someone who was or felt in charge in some way, perhaps being some sort of leader or shepherd to the community. The story ended with the 12th-house Pluto-Venus image of losing everything. He said it might be difficult for me to want to have a community or a family again after such loss, and he said many other things that resonated deeply with emotions and sensations that up to that point had not found words. For a few years I periodically listened to the recording and often spent time with the themes.

At the time of the workshop reading I was living in Los Angeles, a place I found extremely stressful in which to be. My move to Tucson in 2009 was to unwind and destress enough to be able to write the books that had been organizing themselves in my head for a few years. LA was just not a place in which I could breathe freely and relax under any circumstances. I also had blocks regarding certain LA place and street names and in general found it very difficult to understand why I was guided to live there.[7] I knew it could be fun and watched a lot of people enjoy themselves but I had a giant chip on my shoulder about living there. I also felt that I couldn't move to another place. In fact I had intended and planned two moves out of LA within the first year of my arrival and each completely fell through in weird ways. I ended up accepting that I was supposed to be there and I didn't try to move again until I sensed it was time and I landed in Tucson in 2009.

---

[7] See *Seeing Through Spiritual Eyes: A Memoir of Intuitive Awakening* for the complete story on that move and what resulted.

After leaving LA I drove through it twice on my own, going out on and returning from a channeling and lecture tour in July of 2011. I would get scrambled an hour outside of LA and feel stress and anxiety at the feelings rising up within me from being in the area, just as when I had lived there. Many parts of me would leave my body and I wasn't sure I'd be able to keep driving just to get through it. It was draining and exhausting. While I was fine with not wanting to live there I didn't like the idea that I was unable even to drive through or visit. On that 2011 tour I was able to discern that it must be a past-life situation but I had no idea what needed resolution and/or healing. Upon arriving home I felt confident that it could be healed even as I didn't know what that would look like. Prior to that I was simply blindsided by the feelings that arose when there. The feeling was of dread that would build because something awful was true, something terrible was real and I see that I didn't want to know what it was. I had the sense that it might be too much to deal with.

A few weeks after the tour J. moved to Tucson from the Midwest. I had an invitation to return to Yakima, Washington to teach a 2-day intensive on emotional healing and changing karma[8] and she agreed to come along. The simplest way to Yakima would be through LA and I told my girlfriend about all of these feelings. We'd had regular contact when I was on tour in July and she

---

[8] The transcript of the intensive is *The Soul's Journey II: Emotional Archaeology*.

witnessed all of it as it unfolded. We agreed to avoid LA on the way to Yakima and travel up through Nevada and Idaho, leaving open the possibility that we could return through Southern California and connect with friends we wanted to see there. I told her I didn't want to be the one driving through LA if we went that way and so I asked her to do it and she was amenable. We did choose to return to Tucson via LA and when the day came, with her driving into the city I was stressed and became exhausted, as usual, but since she was driving we got to our friends' homes on schedule.

I took her to my favorite local hiking spot, Temescal Canyon. There are steep climbs on both sides of the trail with the top portion traveling in part along the ridge, offering an opportunity for great views of a large part of the LA area. In addition to the ocean-side views of the water to the West and Santa Monica and Venice to the South, depending on the weather you might see all the way to downtown to the South East and Torrance to the South. At the top I stopped to take in my favorite view from the trail – perhaps my favorite spot in the LA area – and noticed that the greenery had grown somewhat in the 2+ years since I'd been there. It looked just different enough to mask the golden roof top of the Self-Realization Fellowship, a well-known marker for me from that vantage point. But as I looked and saw other familiar sights I had this sense that I was home. I heard a part of me say quietly with a recognition that brought peace, "This is my home."

Acknowledging that shifted something deep under the surface. I felt relief that it was okay to admit that LA is my home after 6 years rather unhappily living there and 2 years elsewhere dreading having to return to the area. Over the next almost hour I continued with the thing internally shifting and I did speak with J. about it a bit. I felt vulnerable in a way I had not before experienced, tender and soft in a way that was new. I asked her to snap a photo of me to capture this part of me on film.[9] I figured that I looked more vulnerable than usual and was showing a part of me that doesn't come to the surface that often if at all. Like many other-life parts or bleed-throughs that have a difficult story to tell, it had existed under the surface of conscious awareness but routinely piped up with emotional reactions to certain situations and dynamics in my life. It is very common to carry multiple parts in this way without knowing who they are or what has happened to them. We simply feel what they feel and we assume that those feelings are who we are as opposed to a part of our energy field and consciousness. The process I've undertaken for the last decade to learn to become grounded has enabled me to be able to discern such other-life parts with whom I share karma and an association of soul.

I began to understand that what was happening was that a life associated with my soul on another part of the timeline was making itself known – a bleed-through was coming to the surface. It is a person who lives in a native

---

[9] This photo appears in the About the Author section following the text.

community in the LA area on another part of the Earth timeline and witnesses the catastrophic destruction of his village and community including all the people he knows and loves. He is imprinted with the feeling that everyone loved is dead and because of this there's little point to do much of anything. In the end he feels that life itself has betrayed him. It wasn't just that he lost loved ones but that he lost all of them in a gruesome way in front of his eyes and in a matter of minutes. They are slaughtered and he sees enough of them killed and lying dead to imprint him with shock and sadness to the point that he can't come out of it. He doesn't know what to do with the experience and he dies soon after. Perhaps that was in the same day and perhaps not – I do not have a sense of whether he lived much beyond the massacre.

As I processed all of these images and feelings I came to understand that I had been guided to live in LA so that I could grow to be able to heal this other-life pain. It became clear that because of my stressed and somewhat consistently stunned reaction to being there, though, it couldn't happen until after I moved out of the city. Remember the giant chip on my shoulder to do with living there? It had much to do with trying to keep out of conscious awareness the awful feelings of loss and despair that had been imprinted in that other life. As I look back on it now I sense that other parts of me would have not been able to cope with the vision of needless loss and senseless grief that he presents when he surfaces. With this bleed-through finally communicating openly with me

– at last coming to the surface to share his story – I realized that I now had words and context for a sadness and loneliness I had carried my whole life. Many times it manifests as not staying connected to people I love and I think is in part a protection mechanism to prevent a repeat of my attachment to them so that when they die, I won't be quite as crushed.

Pluto with Venus conjunct it can indicate karmic memories of loss in any chart. In Libra we can add in that the loss has lead to karmic beliefs about a lack of fairness and perhaps being unable to continue without those loved ones. That they are in the 12th house indicates the possibility that the loss was overwhelming, the theme that Steve mentioned in my reading that seemed to portend that I would need to learn to deal with intense loss to heal my Pluto stuff. It is true that everyone experiences loss but some of us don't learn effective means to deal with it. Even when we do we can find the loss of a group of loved ones in the same event such as the story told here simply too much to deal with. My sense is that there are likely a number of parts of me along the Earth timeline who do not know the least thing about dealing with loss and as you will read in the next chapter, it is something I work on regularly in my current relationship with J.

Now I'm faced with learning to deal with this loss on the other part of the timeline. Sometimes I think it's unfair that I have to deal with something that is not in my own personal experience. As noted above we all tend to identify with our other-life emotions until we learn to differentiate them from our experiences and reactions to experiences. I had felt that grief and it was out of all proportion to what I had experienced in this life as Tom Jacobs. Adapting to a view of a human as consciousness that exists across time but anchored in multiple places on the timeline I've been able to step away from feeling that it is unfair that I have to do this – or that I am invited to do it and I am accepting that invitation. Often it feels to me that I can't be happy here and now if I don't learn to deal with it and so I do what I can to stay open and willing. So many situations bring these feelings up, though, and it takes a lot of energy to work with and continue life as normally as possible. A movie or play in which a long-lost family member returns to a loved one cracks me open, as does any story of multiple family members dying at the same time. To those who know me it would seem sometimes that I myself have experienced a tragic loss – I withdraw at times and exhibit depressive states just as someone who has survived a senseless tragedy like the one described above. But that is not my life. I am dealing with emotional imprints from another part of the timeline so that I can be free to enjoy being me here and now.

A number of existing issues related to fears about losing relationships and being unsure how to connect with people and feel close to them became clearer. That sense of grief and loss that has surfaced at different times in my life and now and then can take over. Sometimes at the end of a relationship I have gone into a despair that I figure probably borders on extreme and imbalanced and have to work to come back to center. This man has lost everyone he loved but almost more importantly he felt responsible for them and wasn't able to protect them. Steve Forrest's image in my mini-reading of a native village being decimated by an invading, technologically superior force made sense and in fact fit closely with what I was feeling. The memory of who has done this is somewhat vague but this man feels the overwhelm and so I do, too. It's the sense of being so completely outgunned and you don't have a chance. It makes a person wonder about the intentions and motivations of life and in me this bred a persistent sadness that took a lot of energy to stay connected to. This part of me didn't know anything else – it was what seemed true at the time and he was at a loss to ascribe any other meaning to it.

This kind of situation of living in the 12th house through learning about loss and being overwhelmed can leave someone with Mars-Uranus in the 1st house hesitant to assert himself. The belief goes that if you are going to be overwhelmed by life (and the feeling of it from the other life has been with me all during this life as though happening in this moment) then why bother taking action? What is the point of self-interested decision-making to assert yourself if life is just going to take everything away for no good reason? Why do anything positive and proactive if you're just going to be punished for something you don't know you did? As a result I've found my Mars-Uranus conjunction in the 1st house difficult to come to terms with. The death threats described in "A Youth" above are evidence of the vacuum I created for Mars energy to rush in suddenly (conjunct Uranus) when I was not asserting myself. Remember that if you don't use an energy in your field (chart) then you can create a vacuum and it will come to you in ways that you probably would not choose or appreciate. When I began learning about managing my energy based in chart signatures in order to eliminate such vacuums my first thought was that the whole thing was a sick game: You avoid making noise and asserting yourself so life doesn't step on you and then life comes rushing in to step on you anyway. It took a few years of getting and remaining grounded to work through that disempowered and assumptive reaction and to be okay with continuing with all this other-life processing.

Separately I've learned through different associations that I have an other-life connection with Chumash peoples, a tribal group located around the Ventura, California area. The first was with the girlfriend from the "A Man Who Would Cherish A Woman" chapter, A. One of our first dates was a day trip to Ventura and I mentioned to her that I had troubles getting lost when going there. While we were there she saw the energetic/consciousness effect on me of being there and insisted we go back soon and figure out what the issue was. Her intuition told her that this was something deep that I needed to resolve. In that area north of LA I would get confused and find it hard to be in my body (much more so than in LA at any time) and this would lead to frustration from and anger at the confusion because driving was difficult and being grounded and cogent were nearly impossible. A few weeks later we did go back and this time without a plan, seeing where the day would lead us. We were drawn immediately to the local history museum downtown and I had a pretty significant emotional release in the area with the Chumash exhibits. She held me and I cried quietly for what seemed a long time, until it felt complete. That was the beginning of a long process of release of those old emotions that is ongoing.

The 2nd connection with this tribal group came when I was invited to a sweat lodge in a native camp outside Ojai, California. The couple who run the sweat are Lakota and relocated to Ojai from the Great Plains but in the lodge I felt at home and as though I could finally start to really get grounded and relax. I was invited by a friend at the time and the event coincided exactly with a transit of the Moon to my 7th house Vertex in Taurus. Finally getting deeply grounded to the Earth through an invitation by a friend to a sweat lodge in the mountains seemed appropriate for it! I had recently begun paying attention to transits to the Vertex to understand more about its potential role in the chart and this event convinced me. It wasn't until I got home that I realized the Moon was there that night.

The 3rd connection was the second place I lived in Tucson. The landlady is ¾ Chumash and I felt a kin connection with her. It seemed to tie together the previous experiences and kept me connected to that history, as I'd moved away from easy access to Ojai. I did sweats there perhaps only 5 times but felt that it was my community and I always felt happy and safe when there. I remain on its email list so I can keep abreast of what is happening there.

The 4th connection was a shaman I knew and did trades with in LA. Her spiritual heritage was connected to the Chumash grandmothers and I recognized the familiar energy and comforting connection. We seemed to recognize each other energetically when we met and I really enjoyed working with her.

As I tied together the stories above in writing for the first time just now, I remembered a 5th connection. Just after graduating high school in 1991 I became close to a girl I'd gone to school with, two years younger than me. We'd been running in the same circles more or less but suddenly there was a connection. It was friendly but close and we held hands, feeling good being with each other. There was absolutely no romance involved but I'm sure others thought there must be with the hand-holding. This unfolded when were in Wisconsin in the early Summer for a music camp. When we returned home her parents told her that they had decided to move to Ventura. She and her sister were surprised but plans were underway and later in the Summer it happened. My mom, sister, and I had just moved to a town about an hour away from where I had graduated high school and I just wanted to be closer to my friend. I was sad that she was moving so far away – California seemed like 100 worlds away – and I made at least one trip to my former town to see her before her family moved. We exchanged letters during that time and kept in touch after she moved but when that happened I became – depressed? Maybe morose is the word. I just longed for my friend. I'm not sure I told anyone what I was really feeling but I'm sure my family could tell I was somewhat depressed. During that Summer I drew to work out the feelings I was having and in that collection of images there are several depictions of feelings of loneliness and loss. I think this was the first time that this other-life situation began to bleed through so that I had conscious awareness of the feelings, instead of simply trying to avoid triggering and feeling them. I went into a deep place within that Summer and accessed some spots new to me at that stage.

Writing the other stories out a few minutes ago I began to connect that feeling of loss with the loss of the native man in the LA area on another part of the timeline. My friend didn't feel necessarily like family and she didn't feel like a love interest – as I mentioned, there was simply no romantic interest between us – but I felt connected to her in a deep way and it made me feel more at home in the world. In the last couple of years we've connected through a social media site and have exchanged a few messages. I no longer feel any sense of longing or loss when I think of or interact with her. I believe that the experience was a sort of precursor to me being drawn to live in Los Angeles in order to heal these painful issues from this other place on the timeline. I do not know if my friend believes in or has any interest in reincarnation but I believe strongly that her family moved to Ventura because she at least (though probably more members of the family) needed to be there again, too, to have the chance to make peace with living there by making it home once again.

Since the hike in September of 2011 described above I've been able to connect the dots between this kind of story and a number of relationships in this life that have been important to me. Now and then I identify someone I love in this life whom I sense was someone I lost in that other life. A dear friend of mine I met in college is one of them and I had an immediate and strong reaction when she told me that she was pregnant. I remembered that in the other life she was a child when the village was raided and destroyed. She wanted to grow up and have children and wasn't able to because of the whole massacre dealio. While she was pregnant I confronted the pain of losing her even as I was able to talk to and once see her. When it was time for the baby to be born I experienced some fear about meeting the child because I suspected I would look in her eyes and know that she is one of the ones that I lost. I imagined it might be overwhelming. I realized that I needed to heal this and was excited to visit their city after the baby was born. The parents decided to in a sense circle the wagons and were not open to having visitors for a while. I felt crushed. It had nothing to do with them – they of course should do what they feel is right for them – but I couldn't help but feel that I needed see them with their baby in order for me to make peace with some of the horrific events of this other life of losing everything. I needed to see that joy and happiness can happen again, and apparently I thought I needed to see their human selves huddled around in a group hug in order to be able to open to the idea

Separately I do fear the loss of loved ones except, ironically, my family. I appreciate my mother and will miss her after she passes but I don't fear her death. The same with my sister. My father passed away 5 years ago as of this writing and I didn't fear his passing, either. But with certain friends and lovers I do fear this.

Regarding other themes of this bleed-through's life I also feel a bit burned out on being in charge of things. I had some leadership positions from junior high through the end of college and I always felt like I shouldn't bother, that there was nothing that I really had to offer. Once in office or in the position I periodically had a generalized feeling that none of it mattered and I shouldn't be trying to get anything useful done because in the end, nothing matters. After all, everything will be destroyed horrifically and there's no point in creating community or bothering with anything. Now this would come up after I got elected or appointed! On one level I wanted to do the things but had an underlying sense that none of it really mattered.

Prior to my relationship with A. I don't think my heart was very available. Looking back I am not sure I was ever very present with anyone. My brain was and sometimes my heart was but I wasn't there as a complete, whole person with all parts of me available. There was too much grief and sadness under the surface that not only did I not want to feel and deal with but I was pretty sure no one else would want to be around or deal with either. My ability to work with feelings of loss and grief now while being in relationship is stronger but I do still have some challenges, as you'll read about in the next chapter.

It is prevalent in New Age teachings to value and work on opening the heart. Channeling Ascended Master Djehuty regarding 2012 wherein he offered me tools to teach people to heal Chiron issues[10] I saw that if we are to live heart-centered lives – one of his invitations if we are to evolve as individuals and as a species – we must deal with any resistance to opening our hearts and heal and transform the energies we carry there from the past. We can become attached to all manner of pain and suffering and other sorts of emotions. When this happens we can develop identities surrounding them, storing the emotions (energetic imprints) in our fields and attaching beliefs to what they mean and why the original events that inspired them occurred. Opening the heart can be a daunting task if we do not know how to deal with what we've been carrying there. Since early 2008 this has been the focus of my work and I've been able to develop a number of tools through meditation, energy work, soul fragment retrieval and integration, and interpreting birth charts to support this process.

My situation described above is not the norm. With Pluto-Venus in the 12th house – a house traditionally related to loss and difficulty – I perhaps have experienced

---

[10] The result is the book *Chiron, 2012, and the Aquarian Age: The Key and How to Use It.*

more loss than other people as part of my soul journey to learn about letting go and adapting to how the universe works. But maybe it is instead true that I have simply not learned to deal effectively with loss when it happens as it in fact does to everyone. With this 12th-house signature each is equally possible. Whatever loss is experienced can lead various mes along the Earth timeline to feel a deep chasm in my entire being – if I let it. If I believe that life is hopeless and not worth having faith in then this can lead to feeling bereft, depressive, full of despair, and not invested in being alive. This tendency that has surfaced at times in my life is in direct conflict with my Jupiterian optimism and it can leave me feeling and seeming manic. I know there's no clinical diagnosis of mental imbalance or illness waiting for me because I can trace the sources across the Earth timeline and effectively heal and transform the emotional issues other manifestations of my soul experience on their spots on the timeline. But it's a trip being me, emotionally speaking.

This story not in the least meant to inspire a "poor Tom" thing but to contribute to an explanation of how some of these multilife processes work. Instead of feeling sorry for myself I do what I can to work with the energies and emotions in me that I find unresolved. When I refer to my personal karmic stories in readings and when teaching I seek to impress upon those hearing them that there is a reality of living on Earth that provides experiences that are difficult to handle and process emotionally but that we can learn to hold space within us for processing and moving through them. Being willing to open the heart in order to feel what is stored in one's energy field is the first step of being able to do so.

The pain and grief of this part of my soul's consciousness is triggered often. It is one of those in this book, with the one described in the latter part of the next chapter, that presents the most difficulty on a regular basis. Honestly, I don't know what it will take to heal the pain. What I'm working on now is being willing to feel it – let the part of self come to the surface – and stay grounded enough to be a good friend to him. He has a lot of crap to cry out, though! He's not the kind of friend I would invite over to do something fun. He's the kind of friend having a hard decade and who needs a lot of tender support.

Two Slaves

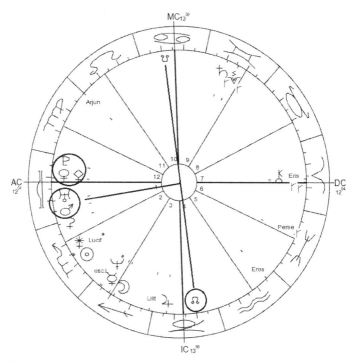

Covered in this chapter: Pluto-Venus in Libra/12th, Mars-Uranus in Libra/1st square the nodes, NN in Capricorn/4th.

Roman

The first life as a slave of which I became aware came up because of something rather mundane. I would not have expected any such thing to happen and it was, as I think of it, one of the first sudden recall experiences of another life I had. It came through as an image and emotional state, a sort of snapshot of a moment but I knew that that moment represented a great portion of life.

In LA I picked up a cute little cat named Maya. At one point I decided to begin letting Maya go outside as I had moved to a residential neighborhood with little traffic and I felt it was safe. Where I had lived previously the situation was different and I had decided to keep Maya inside. She had her front claws and I really wanted her instinctive side to be expressed.

You know how cats are until you put your foot down, right? They want what they want and you can appear to be or be reduced to the status of a tool for their gratification. Maya's thing regarding going outside was to at certain times go in and out and in. I had to open the door for her each time and after a few times of this one day toward the beginning of her desire to have a door man, I started to become annoyed. (It was a rental and I couldn't install a car door, which would have been the ideal solution.) My annoyance escalated into a raw impatience and then, finally, anger. She kept demanding it even as I told her I was done and then I had the flash of the memory from the other part of the timeline and said to her with some Scorpionic fire, "I am not your door slave!"

The impression that came was of standing in front of a door with nothing to do but open it for other people. I knew I am in front of a home and that it is my job to do this. Then I realized that this person is a slave and his job is to open and close the door of this well-appointed home of a wealthy family. He feels humiliated and his self-esteem could not be lower. He is all but checked out mentally and emotionally and in his body just enough to be able to perform this function.

I realized that he is in fact tied to a post near the door. I do not know if this was always the case or if he is being punished but in this sense-image he has a collar around his neck and is tied to this place. There is no room for imagination and none for laughter. There is pretty much nothing but this life of servitude and it is humiliating.

My natal chart features Uranus-Mars in the 1st house in Libra square the nodal axis, telling me that there are lives of my soul in which freedom and the ability and space to express desire and will are issues. In some lives it will likely be overexpressed and in others underexpressed (remember that it is the nature of a square to the nodes to explore extremes of expression to find the right size, use, and direction of expression). A life of slavery makes sense given the theme of Pluto in the 12th, as well, as this indicates a need to learn to be of service and surrender and slavery is a way that some souls get their humans to learn to go with the flow. It is awful and limiting and it can, yes, be full of abuse and other horrible experiences but it is one route that souls choose for their humans to learn one side of surrender.

When I recall this young man I notice how different is his physique from mine. The energy in his body and field is muted and mine is most definitely not. He is around two inches shorter than I am and weighs less. He has a slighter frame and I feel it immediately in the width of his shoulders relative to my broader shoulders. Emotionally speaking he carries a level of resolve to his circumstances that is really just sad to me – he feels defeated and resigned to it. I relate to the feeling of being trapped in certain circumstances and in this life I've had to learn how to work with my spirit guides and ascended masters while not assuming that they are in charge, as though I am a slave to what other, powerful beings want and expect of me. In some ways, in fact, a lot of this life as Tom Jacobs is about coming out the mindset of slavery. At times I have felt trapped in whatever is going on around me and that there is no point in trying to change anything for the better. The belief at those times that surfaces is that no one's listening and no one cares what you're experiencing as long as you are producing what they expect you to produce.

This in fact has been an issue with the books I've published whether written or channeled. It has happened that when I have an idea for something it usually doesn't seem to work out for one or many reasons. When a guide or Djehuty, et al. suggest a project, however, then the doors fly open and I have limitless energy. Circumstances align themselves to support me in finishing the work. For instance when I choose a topic my schedule fills and when I do what I'm asked by spirit to do then it clears and I can focus on the project. I have some idea of the lesson here but my process is ongoing. It seems related directly to the lives of slavery described in this chapter and, likely, other lives of which I'm not yet aware. My soul intends that I learn about surrender (Pluto in the 12th house) while expressing will (Mars-Uranus in the 1st house). Often I see this as an invitation to learn to align personal will with Divine will and I perceive I do this because I do not begrudge the projects that are suggested to me. Yet often there is still a tinge of, "But what about what *I* want?" After all, these works can help people and I am grateful for the chance to be a channel, conduit, and organizer for those teachings. It's just that I am in the process of learning about how to exercise my will in addition to fulfilling the function of channel and it requires that I unlearn some ideas and beliefs gained through experiences on other parts of the timeline.

19th-Century American

The second of the two stories to include in this chapter involves more memories and emotional waves that surface than in the first. It came to light (this part came to the surface) within days of meeting J. She was a big fan of the Unraveling Karma podcast I produced for several years and that lead her to have a reading with me in August of 2010. In May of 2011 she attended her first meeting of Steve Forrest's Apprenticeship Program and we met for the first time in person. I was the only person on the list of attendees with whom she had had contact previously and so she made a point of introducing herself to me. She accosted me with a giant hug that caught me off guard and we ended up talking a few times over the next couple of days. Before the group dinner on the penultimate day of the program we made each other laugh more than we thought possible, each of us having the most fun we could remember. It was clear a connection was brewing.

The next day was the last of the program and her name came out of the hat for a reading to illustrate the workshop's themes. She asked me to sit with her to help her ground and I did, with some intense material coming up from Steve's reading of her chart. One of the themes was slavery and as I sat there holding her hand at her request to help her ground I started to feel confused about what was happening. I could feel her energy field and I was comfortable with her. Then I would look over and feel tension because she was not supposed to be Caucasian with blonde hair and blue eyes – she was supposed to be brown-skinned with dark hair. She was listening to and drinking in what Steve was sharing with the group about her karmic story and was relying on me to help her stay grounded. I was on the verge of freaking out because most things about the situation were entirely wrong. I remember the feelings of confusion and consternation, the frustration of not understanding what was happening. What I knew was that holding her hand was right and all these other details were somehow wrong. It felt important to be connected to her but all these details were out of place.

During a break we went for a walk down the alley outside the building and talked and hugged. I did feel a reconnection with someone I know in other lives on the Earth timeline but I had no details. After the program finished and people were rushing off to the airport she briefly kissed me once and we each had an energetic awakening. For her it was that energy rushed through her body and woke up her lower chakras and for me, something was stirred and it took two days to understand what it was.

We talked on the phone the next morning as I made my way back to Tucson and she was again at home. She talked as though we would have much time to share things and be together and I was pretty much shell-shocked because what was stirred was not yet clear. I kept thinking that something was right but something else was off and I didn't know what to do. J. was familiar with me on the phone and I tried not to be distant but I was skeptical.

The day after I arrived back in Tucson it all came to light. I remember it was after sunset and I was at my computer trying to work these things out. I might have been recording an audio letter for her even though I was pretty sure we'd talk daily for a while – at times I couldn't wait and had to say the thing right away even if we were going to speak in a few hours. I had the visceral and emotional knowing that we are family and that I had to help her. I felt into that and saw that in a bunch of lives she isn't looked out for and nurtured by her families in a certain way and that it was now time for her family to step up and help her.[11] At this time she was in a marriage and living a life that in many ways did not suit her and I felt that I had to take her in to my home and protect her. As I felt into these feelings I tapped in to a slave in the American South in the early-mid 19th century who couldn't look out for and protect her as his wife. I had a welling up of loving, pained, and sorrowful feelings about having lost her and feeling that I couldn't do anything to help her. I knew that she is being abused in many ways by the slave owner in that other life including numerous rapes. I felt that in that time she is my wife but I can do nothing to protect her. On that other part of the timeline that me is beaten as a result of his attitude and behavior and by the time of the formation of these emotional memories that were spilling up to the surface and washing over me, this man feels utterly defeated. He has lost her to death after a life of losing her to abuse and in no way has he been able to help her.

I felt strongly that in this life I had to help her as J. The feeling filled me and I started to feel sharp intellectually and emotionally. I saw that it was time for me to spring into action and help her and I felt entirely

[11] This would be part of the souls' contracts with each other. From the human point of view we can seem or be abandoned or left behind but such experiences are always sourced in the loving support souls offer each other while incarnated as humans. This can be painful but is a marker of the love between souls. I felt not the wisdom of the soul contracts of this family group but the urge of a human on another part of the timeline to remedy a situation created by humans that had caused J. pain.

sane. It was then that I started telling her that I was completely sane about her. We often feel lit up for new love interests such that we say that we're crazy for the other person but I felt absolutely sane because of the connection, as though I had snapped out of a lifetime of confused and crazy and finally felt like I was doing things right.

When we spoke next I poured out this story to her and I made a commitment to myself to do whatever was necessary to help her get into a new way of life. I sensed that she felt controlled where she was living and she confirmed it. She said it wasn't that her husband was a bad man but that the dynamic between them engendered some unhealthy patterns. She loved him and still does but living there in that situation caused her to feel trapped and unable to fully be herself. I told her she should move in with me and let me help her get on her feet in a new city. We talked extensively about it over the next few months and she processed the prospect of a major life transition.

About 2½ weeks after we met she flew to Tucson for 5 days to start to get to know me in person. We had a blast and knew something important was happening. In mid-July she met me in Portland for a week while I was on the channeling and lecture tour. We each knew on that trip that we were going to be together and that she would end her marriage and move to Tucson to be with me.

Now, all of this was surreal to say the least. I had to deal with the end of 4 years of isolated bachelorhood and she had to deal with the end of 9 years of being with someone she loved but needed to leave. And there were other things from her past coming up to be dealt with plus the logistics of uprooting and a major move coupled with the emotional process with her then husband. Yet all the time I knew I was doing what needed to be done by opening my home to her and offering her support and impetus to make a major life move.

Emotionally I was recovering the willingness to take a stand and believe that what I want and what is important to me matters. More than once in conversation with J. I adopted a rock-solid position that action had to be taken and when she produced questions and doubts about the unknown and the complexities of all the processes mentioned in the paragraph above, I dug deep for the assuredness and confidence that we could work through anything that came up. I told her as many times as she needed to hear it that we could and would work through anything that came up. I told her this was right even though difficult and she agreed.

One detail was that I was living at the time in a one-bedroom house that was under 450 square feet. It was a bit of a bachelor pad but really a weird sort of bachelor shack and hidey-hole that I had chosen because it would suit and support the writing and publishing of books. I had it set up essentially as a writing studio with a bed. She had more possessions than she thought might fit in this tiny house with both of us living there. She worried about it and I told her we'd figure it out. I didn't have the funds to get a bigger place yet and she wasn't earning money at the time so I chose to have confidence that it would work out. The most important thing in my mind was to get her from Kansas to Tucson and into my house and arms. This me from another life was regaining the ability to be strong for a loved one who needed support and it brought out in me the ability to heal this slave's lifetime of disempowerment and feeling everything about me and what I found important was meaningless.

I flew to Kansas to help her move. She was understandably having a hard time leaving but knew she needed to do it. Over the following few months I kept the faith that this was best even as we almost couldn't move or breathe in the tiny house with her stuff stacked to the ceiling. I had to rent a room in a neighboring house in which to write and work because suddenly my studio and office was filled with boxes of stuff and a woman dealing with a difficult, major life transition.

In the first few weeks following her move another phase to healing this other manifestation of my soul began. For a few months I woke up almost each day with the feeling in my biceps that I was about to have charley horses. I was familiar with the feeling of the moment before I get them and had trained myself to freeze in order to stave them off. Over the years I'd had them from time to time in my legs and usually during sleep – waking up just in time to stop the pain – but never in my biceps. This continued and I tried to feel into it for a few weeks but got nothing. I also began to have the sense memory of carrying her dead body in my arms and I think this inspired me to try to keep some of the deeper feelings related to the charley horses at bay. I wasn't sure I could deal with opening to feeling all of that without editing them or controlling the flow.

Then there followed a period during which I would wake up feeling simultaneously sad and happy, feeling crushed but also being so very thrilled that J. was with me. She would be sleeping next to me and I would be running this range of feelings and not know how to make sense of or what to do with them. After a few weeks of that I woke up being sure that she was dead but then realizing that she wasn't; that she was right there with me. I cried quite a bit first from the sadness and then it would shift momentarily into tears of joy that she was there. This continued for months and once I had words for it I told her about it. She was understanding and loved that I loved waking up with her. I told her often how happy I was that she wanted to be with me and moved so far while changing her life to be my partner.

But all this time I was trying to hold back the full force of the feelings. One morning when the words began lining themselves up and I felt brave and asked her if I could talk through it in case that would help my aching heart and arms get a rest from the drama, and she was open. I cried and cried and gripped her, telling that I miss her – in the present tense. I let this part of self from the other part of the timeline speak through me. After perhaps 3 or more months of dancing around the grief and sadness from losing her I gave in and articulated everything. I told her again and again how much I miss her and I held her tightly and cried and kissed her and had the experience of opening this other-life part of me to begin to release those pent-up feelings from that other part of the timeline. Since then I've been experiencing more of this but with less urgency. Now in the mornings I often have the sense that she is dead but that I get to be with her again and I wake up affectionate and loving, wanting her to be aware of all the adoration and appreciation I feel. In the morning is when this other-life part of me is most present. I think this is because these other-life connections we have to our souls' manifestations on other parts of the Earth timeline occur through our energetic bodies. When I get out of bed in the morning I tend to get my mind in gear to accomplish the day I've planned and this to some degree disconnects me from a direct experience of mes on other parts of the timeline. There are days when I'm processing this stuff or other stuff and simply cannot get to work – cannot get my mind in gear – and I've learned to flow with it. For me, processing emotions is in being with them and maintaining consciousness of the part of self that is speaking whether this is an inner kid or a manifestation of soul from another part of the timeline.

I know that with J. a major opportunity exists for me to deal with the reality of death – of losing a loved one – and in appreciating the time that we have together. I am still in process with this part of my consciousness and I deal with these issues on a regular basis. There are weeks here and there during which I'm present with her and not grieving her past and future deaths and other weeks when every time I look at her part of me wants to cry buckets, hold her, and tell her I love her dearly and want the best for her, etc. Think of all the things you might regret not telling your lover or spouse if you are disempowered enough to fail to say anything before he or she died and then wake up each day with him or her there and have a second chance. There are many days that feel like second chances with J. and even as I am learning to grieve the past I am also learning to appreciate the present moment. Each time I think of it the faucet of emotion turns on, and that tells me that there is still much to process and release.

A few years ago I had a deep emotional connection with a woman I knew as a wife of mine on another part of the timeline. I sensed that life there is pretty straightforward and that we are happy together with children. When I met her in late 2004 I had been connecting with the feeling of life being full of unhappiness. Through my relationship with her was able to remember a feeling of being happy. I also remembered having children with her in that other live and not seeing any awful disaster befall me, us, or them. That dynamic was part of the process of beginning to let go of the sense of loss described in the above chapter "A Man Who Loses Everything" and this one concerning a life with J. So now I have that memory inside, of being happy and that there is nothing wrong. I can add to it that I get a second chance with a woman I love dearly.

With J. it is also true that I have relationships with different parts of her. As in most relationships some of her behaviors make me nuts and some of mine do the same to her. But I see her primarily as my family and that I have the opportunity to do something loving and supportive for someone in my family who felt lost to me and lost in general (referencing the feeling that arose just after meeting her that our family had not stood by her and that I needed to now in order to help her and heal the family system). Since all of this has occurred I also have accessed a memory of being J.'s father, loving and so proud of her as a young woman and my daughter in another life. There is also a memory of being energetically joined at the hip as sisters. An intuitive friend and colleague of mine described the father-daughter and twin sister lives to me during a session after J. and I met and it makes a lot of sense. We have much fun and love playing together but the father-daughter dynamic also sometimes come out. I intentionally don't instruct her or criticize her but I do sometimes see her as a kid when she's in fact older than I am and in some areas of life has notably more experience and wisdom. I'm sure at times she sees me as a kid, too! We each admit to being multidimensional and who knows what other-life bleed throughs might be working through our relationship.

Regarding the 19th century slave life described above, I'm clear that recovering my ability to stand up for something I believe in (Mars-Uranus in the 1st house), standing by family members (North Node in Capricorn/4th house), and learning to grieve and release (Pluto-Venus in Libra/12th house) present ongoing challenges. J. is a teacher for me in holding space for other-life parts of me to come forward and speak what they are feeling as well as for me to step up to the difficulty of growth in all three areas of life. Far from being depressing in the end, waking up most mornings with grief in fact inspires much more appreciation for the time that we have together. I try to take as many opportunities as I can to express my appreciation and affection for her because life is too short to keep quiet about it. I have a lot of lost time to make up for.

Three Church Men

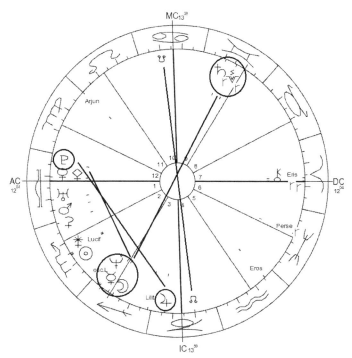

Covered in this chapter: Pluto in the 12th square Jupiter in Capricorn/3rd, SN ruler Moon in Sagittarius/3rd conjunct Neptune-Mercury and opposing Saturn-Vesta in Gemini/9th, SN ruler stellium sextile Pluto-Venus.

Spreading the Word

My awareness of this person living on another part of the timeline began to seep in indirectly about the time I became aware of the Roman door slave described above. It was later that I understood more about the dynamics of his life and so I'm situating this chapter here to reflect the time it took for the full story to unfold in my awareness.

It began when I lived in LA and started teaching at a metaphysical center in Anaheim. I contacted them and sent some info about me, proposing some workshops, and they were interested. I set up perhaps 4 events over a 6-month period but was there only 3 events as one workshop had no sign-ups and I didn't bother making the drive just in case someone came in at the last minute. I was driving my Honda Nighthawk 250 motorcycle on surface streets from LA to Anaheim and it was quite a time investment. The engine was small and didn't have a lot of power to make me feel good riding it on the highway. Sometimes it felt like a suped-up lawnmower with brakes and a headlight and sometimes it sounded like that, too.

In all 3 of the workshops I taught the student numbers were small. In two there were two students and in the other just one. Each of these people had backgrounds in religion before their metaphysical explorations and were in varying stages of deconditioning from them. I found myself teaching about soul, my brand of evolutionary astrology, and reframing a vision of past lives to these people. For most it was in direct conflict with ideas they had been exposed to whether through old-timey doctrine or new-agey teachings. In each of these workshops I found myself working really hard to get through these metaphysical points, working harder than I had done with anyone else whether in classes elsewhere or in one-on-one sessions. It had nothing to do with the people involved but the karmic contracts in play. In other words it wasn't a lack of intelligence or interest on their part that caused me to have to work harder but some synchronistic chemistry between the souls involved.

The last workshop –with one student – was when I saw what was going on. I often use students' charts when teaching to make the principles come to life. I do this so that they deeply understand the teachings but also so that they go home with a deeper understanding of him- or herself. This man has his South Node in Sagittarius, the sign of the believer. The ruler Jupiter was also in Sagittarius, making for a double indication that growth in this life depends on shedding old and past ideas almost no matter what they are. He needs to move into new paradigms (Gemini North Node) and make sure he isn't wearing blinders in any part of life.

I found myself unable to get through to him because of the strength of his beliefs. He had told me he was raised as a Catholic and I could feel the strength of his convictions. While working with him and straining to invent new ways to convey my material to him so that it would get through, I began to see another life on the timeline, one of working extra hard to indoctrinate this same person into religious teachings. I saw myself leading him in that other life to believe something and in this life to try to begin opening his mind and cease believing in it. I felt joyful as I saw the bigger picture of how we go back and forth with each other over the course of many lives. I saw that we do not always do the same thing or have the same effect on each other but that we in each life present to each other an opportunity to grow and change. Based on what is happening at the time that we meet the effects we can have on each other can go one way or the other but we always have the chance to impact each other. For instance if this man had come into the class refusing to believe in anything I would still seek to have an effect on him because of the nature of our contract together. Due to his position about belief in that case it might be to inspire him to trust believing in his own Divine nature, his intuition, or the notion that the universe is a loving place and that we can learn to cocreate with universal energies. As it was I tried to open his mind to a perspective on soul around which a mind trained by Catholicism might not be expected to be comfortable wrapping itself.

This dynamic was echoed over the following few years with clients who had been raised or trained in religious veins. I repeatedly found myself sharing with such people the vision of soul from Ascended Master Djehuty that no existing religion reflects. I watched their minds and hearts open, their imaginations and intuitions come back online, and I felt a sort of redemption after having trained them in other lives to think in a narrow fashion according to a religion's rules. That I had freed myself from something that felt limiting to me enabled me to help others see how to free themselves if that appealed to them. More often than not this comes with clients and students coming from Catholic backgrounds. In this life I was born to and raised in a Reform Jewish environment but I have rarely felt Jewish. Instead I have felt antireligion most of my life until making progress with the judgmental part of myself and learning more about compassion and withholding judgment. My sense is that there are many more other lives on the Earth timeline associated with me that have Catholic themes and realities that need healing and resolving than there are lives as a Jew. I could be wrong about this but it feels that way at this point and has for several years. To be honest, and this is something I do not often share, in this process of recalling and integrating parts of self (other lives) from across the Earth timeline I have recovered many pieces of self that have little patience for victim stances and therefore find it difficult to feel aligned with Judaism. There are also some antisemites in the karmic mix that I've had to educate about living life as me, a life in which I have a deeply observant Orthodox Jewish sister married to a rabbi and have other family members involved in Judaism whom I choose to respect, even if I can't follow suit.

Every time that I open up a person's mind to a different view of reality I recognize that it is all about soul-level contracts to teach and share insights with each other at the right times, in the right contexts, and for the right reasons. I don't teach anything a person is not asking me to teach and I do not expect anyone to want to learn anything they don't want to learn. I see this as a direct reversal of the other-life mindset of proselytizing that goes hand-in-hand with Catholicism. I always get the sense that those lives as a Catholic priest and teacher tend toward a form of zealotry that lends itself well in those personas to a desire to at best change people's minds and at worst brainwash others. My work in this life seeks to make available ideas and teachings that offer a chance to resonate with an inner truth that is about as far away from any sort of doctrine and dogma as you can get. In my chart this can be seen as a shift from the dogmatic and narrow tendencies of a SN ruler in Sagittarius to opening up the Neptunian influence through its conjunction to the SN ruler Moon in a new way. Given that this outer planet is conjunct the SN ruler I will in all of these lives show up as a Neptunian figure but some questions arise: will I be lost in or addicted to my beliefs or will I open up to universal perspectives and align with what I feel is true? Will I let ego get so big I can't admit anything is bigger than me/it or will I admit it and learn to surrender to it, whatever that is? If the thing bigger than me is an institution or a tradition and I surrender to it we can be pretty sure that politics and economics factor in. If instead it is a sense of the divine, then the story is very different. There are lives of my soul in which the human manifestations surrender to different variations of Neptune energy and my present life doing that as a medium and channel is just one possibility.

There are times when I'm speaking, teaching, or on the radio when I feel that I'm preaching. For a few years I've joked about the nested set of soap boxes I drag around with me, just waiting for an excuse to whip one out and get on top of it to say Something Very Important and/or Inspiring. When it feels like I'm preaching I am embarrassed. I think that in other lives at some points I'm teaching things I don't truly believe and this over time would be damaging to anyone. I believe strongly in what I'm doing as Tom Jacobs and I believe in part that this is a direct response to teaching in other lives things behind which I can't fully stand. I have found that what a person is most committed to in any given life can reflect doing the opposite in other lives and feeling something other than good about it. Just as someone can go in one life from an extreme of belief and behavior and do a 180 degree switch to the opposite, it works the same way across time. Remember that emotional memories are shared between many different lives associated with the same soul and that social, economic, religious, filial, etc., conditions in various lives inform and affect the kinds of choices those individual humans make at different points along the timeline. Also remember that there are multiple ways to express each archetypal energy and that it often comes down to choosing one side of a coin over the other in a given thread of life. For instance honesty is the other side of the coin from dishonesty. When the soul chooses this as a theme for the humans associated with it to learn about life, the soul learns what it needs to learn whether honesty or dishonesty is chosen. It is all the same to the soul but your human selves are imprinted by the choices you and those other yous from other places on the timeline make. The resulting feelings about self, other, and the event stay with you in many lives.

In this case, my teaching about higher thought and spirituality is the name of the game. What I perceive is true and how willing I am to align my outward behavior and life with that perceived truth is another story. In this life it seems that I am more or less being authentic and that I have pretty much aligned my outer life to my inner truth.[12] It has been a challenge and, at times, extremely difficult to let go of what my mind has decided must be true in favor of what all of my being vibrates is most definitely true. Perhaps in this life I am balancing out the scales when it comes to my many human choices along the Earth timeline. I do know that I hear from clients, students, and readers frequently that they are using both my written and channeled material and sessions with me to free themselves from limiting ideas picked up and solidified in the past. I do feel that in this life as Tom Jacobs I'm making progress in this way.

---

[12] I write "more or less" authentic and "pretty much aligned" because I have to admit that creative work I crave doing often gets left behind in favor of my metaphysical work. To this point it has seemed much more important to develop these ideas and practices to share with others but I do confront the inner reality that to feel fulfilled as Tom Jacobs much more energy will need to be directed toward creative expression.

The square between Pluto and Jupiter is also relevant here. One level of this can be experienced as a person perceiving being strong through transforming (Pluto) belief (Jupiter). This can come in the form of getting off on convincing others of things whether for good or ill. Being persuasive is a skill that can come from this but we should also see that within the chart holder there can be a tendency to see empowerment through beliefs as a battle. Remember that squares engender friction, pressure, and criticism to change. Plutonian empowerment can at times come at the cost of Jupiterian/Capricornian honesty and forthrightness just as Jupiterian empowerment can at times come at the cost of Plutonian authenticity. This is the nature of the square as it is explored in different contexts over the course of many lives.

A Life High on the Hog

That note leads into the other Catholic priest and teacher story. This side of this way of life that has become apparent in the last few years and I am still working with to shed the past and integrate it into my daily life. It seems that I could not begin to work with this side of me until I had become practiced in self-forgiveness.

At some point living in that small house in Tucson that served as a live/work studio I began to have awareness of a part of me that was embarrassed to enjoy things. My work persona seemed to take over my life and I had a bit of a social life but not much of one. It turns out that a particular spirit guide of mine during that time was tasked with keep me out of relationship. I was lonely and frustrated and felt that life didn't want me to socialize with others. This brought up angry parts determined to enjoy social activities and relationships with the opposite sex and feeling entitled to pleasure as any human would be. After quite a while of working with the frustration and feeling of being forced into life as a hermit I gained some insights about this other life.

At some point while letting this voice speak I had the image of sitting in a well-appointed, luxurious chamber that is part of my living quarters. I am heavy and not very healthy, and have all the food and drink I want and, in fact, can handle. I saw I am an official in the Catholic church and am getting off on living high on the hog. This person has a rather negative view of the community and the world full of Christians that are happily giving their hard-earned money to the church so people like me can enjoy life's finer pleasures and get off on it. This man has no remorse and in fact his moral compass looks like something out of a Salvador Dali painting – melted, warped, and only barely recognizable. These memories came to the surface because he enjoys prostitutes in secret and I was having a period in life in which relationships were not happening. I was consistently guided away from places I knew I could meet like-minded women and when I did happen to meet them they were guided or yanked away from me.[13] I wasn't just horny but I missed the interaction with and touch of a partner. I missed closeness and sensuality as well as sexual expression and for a Scorpio with Pluto-Venus and Mars-Uranus in Libra surrounding the Ascendant, a partner of some kind is pretty much essential for my health on all levels.

This other life seems to center on the pursuit of pleasure and in this life I've been in some ways averse to it. The SN ruler in Sagittarius can indicate someone who seeks pleasure and gratification, and who enjoys life to its fullest whether this is a good thing or not. As I met this persona from the other part of the timeline I saw that some of my patterns with approaching excess and trying to avoid pleasurable things in order to avoid excess in this life are responses to patterns present in other lives. Now, living periods as a sort of ascetic will bring up other-life personas of long-dead monks hoping I don't have to repeat that dry and lonely existence! But experiencing a lot of pleasure can as the converse seem to bring up judgment of living in excess. I'm working to balance these different personas and it is a yet another ongoing process. Parts of me argue that life is about work and the opportunity to offer wonderful, inspirational stuff to others. Other parts of me are worn out from working and want to play and indulge themselves. I seem to be producing quite a lot of work and I know I am learning to relax more and work fewer hours

---

[13] The details of the numerous missed connections are absurd and I've decided not to go into them here.

and for shorter durations, so perhaps I am making progress overall with achieving this balance.

The thing I keep coming back to about this other-life me is being unapologetic about taking advantage of others but in fact Tom Jacobs has felt awful about it. It's not that this other-life guy doesn't know those people and therefore can't put faces on the situation. Rather it's that he sees life as a game of acquisition and he views himself as successful in it because he has toys, pleasures, and fun. This is one kind of human response to having Pluto-Venus in square to Jupiter because it can represent deriving pleasure from receiving from others. One side of this configuration can have a human in certain lives exploring just how much he can get.

Anything he wants to experience is essentially at his beck and call because he has access to money, privilege, and power. When I look at him my judging self tends to think "glutton" but again, it's important to learn the real sort of strength and power that come from acceptance of what has happened and what we have chosen. I can't change the past by judging it, which is to say that I can't change the events he is choosing long ago on the Earth timeline. What I can do is ensure that as he bleeds through to my present awareness I can get clear on the lesson that his life serves in the longer journey of my soul learning what it means, requires, and costs to live lives as a human. Yes, I can take advantage of others – I can convince them to give me things. I could be a fantastic snake-oil salesman or any other kind, actually. But I can also take that skill in influence and align it with my heart, which aligns it with my entire being, something that seems a bit left out in some other lives. When I do that I in fact vibrate something positive and helpful for people. Now I make my living doing spiritual work once again and I often feel like a religious figure without religion but the story is much different this time around. Now my main tasks about this issue include to make sure that I give myself permission to enjoy life as well as to work hard and to judge or fear neither set of activities. I work regularly with the part of me that thinks that all pleasure must lead to trouble.

A Man Who Can Spin Anything

This story is a brief one that in part ties in to the two just described. I have an awareness of how to use information to suit any purpose. It seems to me that this is in modern times the work of advertising but in former times could be categorized as propaganda. My language skills are developed in tandem with a grasp on psychology such that I feel capable of selling anyone anything. I don't feel good about that prospect and I believe that it is sourced in some guilt about spreading religious teachings that I didn't necessarily believe in during some lives. It is difficult at times for me to admit to this anyone outside a few intimates but I carry a part of me that can enjoy being a trickster in the form of playing a game to see if I can convince others to believe or give me things. In the past I

189

did not let this part out much at all but have had to learn to make peace with him and take some cues from him because to a large degree the amount of work I do depends upon marketing – telling people what I do and why they want to consume my services. This part of self is central to my life these days, in fact, for this reason.

The trickster archetype is in my mind central to both advertising and propaganda as both life and buying and selling can be seen as games. In modern culture we are dealing with the psychological, emotional, and material realities of the cycle of acquisition that can lead to a lack of fulfillment. To my mind this has happened on a large scale over a long period of time on this planet in part through the effects of organized religion. A few people here and there start telling others what God wants and in time they are believed, leading to the establishment of an idea and belief pipeline.

Over the millennia we have become primed to being receivers of information. It's come to a head now as we are in transition from the Piscean to the Aquarian Age, during which we cannot help but cease accepting all that trickles down from those who claim or seem to be more spiritual than we are in favor of each individual discerning for him- or herself what is true and aligning with that as a guiding principle. Now when I see people staring blankly at televisions I go a bit nuts because of the energy of blind acceptance and unchecked absorption into consciousness that for me is the amazingly successful result of lifetimes of work to get people to believe things. At those times I have a visceral aversion to being around a television and those who are soaking up all it offers.

This persona came to the surface often over several years as I developed work regarding the Lilith and Lucifer archetypes and wrote draft sections of the book that became *Lilith: Healing the Wild*. Lilith in part represents our relationship to the natural feminine and this came under attack by the mind-based paradigm that created, ushered in, propagated, and maintained patriarchal culture approximately 6,000 years ago. The wild, natural feminine – what might not be consistent and resists control – had to be compartmentalized and spun to be a negative influence outside titillation and procreation along the parameters of the masculine mindset. This was the job of early Jewish thinkers. Lilith as the first woman became the natural target of the distorted and distorting views of the natural wild and the feminine that became entrenched in belief with the rise of Judaism. When Christianity came along its shapers recognized that the feminine was sufficiently demonized and moved on to negatively spin the natural masculine, which is expressed through a doubting mind. Lucifer became demonized as a result to make sure that no one asked hard questions of God and his minions or thought him- or herself better than God to the point of thinking for the self, which is to say thinking outside the controlled and defined lines of that particular religious paradigm.

Working on these archetypal stories and the spiritual-psychological remedies I've developed and use with clients, this persona that sees such things as a game to play came to the surface. This part of me knows that if you understand the political and psychological context you're in you can use information to do anything you like. I see this as related to the SN ruler stellium in Sagittarius sextile Pluto-Venus in the 12th as it gives an ability to work with psychological understanding in order to convince people of things, sometimes tapping into the collective unconsciousness (Pluto-Venus in the 12th house) to make it happen.

You can manipulate some people into loving or hating the point of view that you've chosen to represent. Life itself can be seen from within this mindset as a series of debates in which one person takes a side to get somewhere desired and someone else does the same and, sometimes, neither believes in what they are saying. I do feel that I have the ability to use language and thought in this way but something about debate makes me weary. My major in college was philosophy but the side of me capable of making and engaging in philosophical argument (taking a position and defending it) could not come into play. In some ways I didn't care to verbally work out different positions and in other ways I just was not interested much of the subject matter and couldn't energize myself to be an active part of the department. I learned a lot about thinking and writing and gained practice fleshing out thought into reasoned statements. Yet I didn't have juice for the intellectual rigors of debate and, even, playing devil's advocate in the spirit of uncovering subtleties of thought and its processes. This part of me sees debate as useful only if I have a stake in getting someone else to come over to my point of view. The first three decades of my life were spent looking for a thesis statement or guiding principle in which I could believe. During college I just couldn't mobilize to argue even in an academic context to support my grades! It seemed an empty agenda.

When working on the Lilith and Lucifer archetypes the part of me that is capable of this came forward and acknowledged that the old-time Jews and Christians "played a good game." When I see the world through his eyes I can recognize the wide-spread effects of millennia of spin in religious contexts that have resulted in so many people on the planet unsure about how to decondition from those influences and learn to think for themselves in novel ways. I have the sense that at some points in some lives on the timeline I participated in the campaigns to vilify each of these mythological figures and that at least some of the time those mes did not believe in what they were doing but saw it as a game to achieve some desired goal whether personal, professional, or patriotic.

This is in part associated with using behavior and gestures to win people over to one thing or another. For a lot of my life I have been hesitant to let anything charming come out. Girlfriends and friends have seen this side of me to a degree and one girlfriend commented years ago that I could charm anyone into doing anything. I hadn't realized that I was letting it out but with Venus in Libra on the Libra Ascendant, when in love it might be inevitable that it comes out. I remember being nervous when she said that but upon seeing my reaction she said it was okay for me to be charming. For the last few years I've been exploring that side of me and admittedly with mixed results because I still get nervous at times. There is a part of me that is still resistant to the idea of taking advantage of others through manipulation and, apparently, my willingness to charm is affected by it, too. The SN ruler Moon in Sagittarius/3rd is sextile Venus in Libra/12th, pointing to an ability to use intuition about others to achieve my 3rd-house Sagittarian goals. In the end it all comes down to what I am aligning with when it comes to Pluto in the 12th and the SN ruler conjunct Neptune – is it true or is it something I would like to be true?

Typing that reminded me that after publishing and promoting *Seeing Through Spiritual Eyes: A Memoir of Intuitive Awakening*, for a time I made it unavailable and ceased talking about it. The book in part explains the role of spirit guides in our lives and offers suggestions about learning to work with them. I state in it that guides only work for our highest good and that there are times when we can't see that it's true because of difficult things that might be happening in our lives. I wrote that during such times it is imperative to choose faith that they are helping and not harming us. At one point I learned about the guide who had the job of keeping me out of relationship, for example. I had previously known that she was my "relationship guide" and believed she was helping me find the right relationships and so when I learned the truth I felt deeply betrayed. I pulled the book because I couldn't believe any longer in what I had written even though at the time I had believed it. It seemed disingenuous to teach people something that I was experiencing as untrue. In retrospect I can see how that experience fit with this 3rd church man with the ability to spin and sell things in which he might not believe. After more than a year I made the book available again but have not emphasized it in my marketing. I think I still have a bit of charge about the kind of experiences that spirit guides set up for me to learn. I know deep down that the truth is that they set things up for the human to learn that suit the learning journey of the soul and that these things don't always please the human's personality and heart.

Another Youth

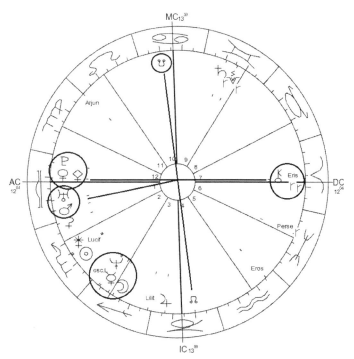

Covered in this chapter: Cancer SN and ruler Moon conjunct Neptune, Pluto-Venus-Pallas Athene in Libra/12ᵗʰ with Venus square the nodal axis, Chiron-Eris in Aries/7ᵗʰ square the nodal axis, Mars-Uranus in Libra/1ˢᵗ square the nodal axis.

At some point along the way while being tutored by Djehuty about soul and its connections to its multilife journey I had begun to figure out something interesting. It seemed that whatever a person was committed to strongly in a given life can represent an attitudinal pendulum swing from the opposite in at least one other life. When we learn as humans how to make choices and deal with the results we sometimes explore extremes of ideas, attitudes, and behaviors. It's normal and to be expected as we try to figure out how to align our personalities with what I call the "inner goodness barometer," the internal sense that right is right and wrong is wrong. Morality can be shaped by ideas but I believe strongly that this inner barometer does not change as we develop and inhabit various belief systems and moral attitudes. There are times in just about all of our lives when we make a choice that goes against what feels right (whether through necessity – for survival – or experimentation, from desire, and/or just to see what will happen). An energetic imprint results that can affect us in many lives. Later in a particular life and in other lives along the Earth timeline we may feel that imprint emotionally whether it comes up as shame, guilt, regret, resentment, anxiety about making choices in one part of life or another, that a desire is dangerous but oh so good, or anything else.

For several years I had been developing various teachings related to goddess archetypes, [14] working to bring an understanding of archetypal processes that differ from myths as social instruction. During this process I had an

---

[14] See *Living Myth: Exploring Archetypal Journeys, Lilith: Healing the Wild*, and *Goddess Past, Present, and Future*.

interesting realization when I saw my choices in this life when it came to how I treated and interacted with women as an extreme. I was able to discern that the other side of it – the negative if it were film – was not gentle or courteous and didn't take into account how they felt. Some of this will be explored in the chapter below titled "A Patriarchal Man" but this emotional imprint deserves its own treatment.

During client sessions and talks I observed myself dispelling the myth of Lilith and teaching the archetype and its emotional/psychological process to others with such passion that I knew something under the surface should be looked into. I figured it was something that likely portrayed behavior that didn't honor the natural feminine in general and women in particular. I do not remember the circumstances that lead to this memory coming to the surface but for a few weeks I asked myself and meditated on what it could be in some other life that would inspire such a pendulum swing if in fact that's what I had been observing. One day I tapped into a feeling of shame and regret, a deep sense of having done something very wrong. I felt into it as I had been learning to do – as you have been reading about – and it wasn't long before I found a shamed, apologetic part of self that had a lot of motivation to try to explain that he was powerless to stop what had happened. He knew it sounded like a justification and he felt there was none but he needed to speak and be heard. Over the following days I felt into him more deeply and found a young man in his teens from several centuries ago who had been out with a handful of friends late one night drinking and causing mild mischief, as it can be perceived boys are wont to do. On the street on the way to the part of town where they lived one of them got the idea to pull a girl into a dark alleyway and one thing lead to another, resulting in a rape. Three of the five boys were involved and this part of me showed me that it was the last thing he expected to happen. He insists that it was happening before he realized what was going down. He is also drunk and regrets having consumed so much alcohol that he couldn't think straight, let alone help the girl and protect her from his friends. I don't get the sense that he or the other boys know her so there was no emotional connection but his normal sense of human empathy was triggered. He feels sorry for the girl, angry with his friends, and stupid and angry with himself for not doing anything to help her. He carries a deep sense of guilt and shame for this experience when he comes through to me. I can tell that he feels shame for the rest of his life and that the boys are not found out to be responsible for the rape. The girl may or may not seek help afterward but none of the boys is identified and punished for what they did.

Prior to this part of self or other-life piece coming directly into conscious awareness I was aware of being somewhat shy around most women and being afraid to express my feelings one way or another to them. I think with Chiron in the 7th house it is natural for me to attract others in general and women in particular who are in need of healing something or who have healing to offer. In

Aries this is in part about sexual desire. Eris in the configuration leads to situations in which when I express desire I can trigger others' insecurities. Think about the numbers of women who have been sexually abused in some way and also those who have made choices regarding their sexual expression about which they at times don't feel good and might judge themselves. Then notice that these are just about the only women you ever meet! (It has seemed this way to me at times in life.) Then the Eris triggering can take place and chaos can ensue as they try to blame or try not to blame me for their Aries-type wounding having been opened up if I act like a man around them, the pain coming to the surface after perhaps years of dormancy. I believe I had in some ways developed some pretty weird approaches to expressing desire for women because I was afraid to hurt them, be too aggressive, be perceived as interested "only in one thing," and afraid to be in a mode of objectifying them and not seeing who they are beyond attractive women who get my internal chemistry-set juices flowing.

A woman I dated in my 20s brought up this issue through her interest in me grabbing her and having my way with her. I cared about her and found her attractive but felt blocked. During an off time in our on-and-off-again relationship she asked me if I remembered a particular moment from months or a year or so prior. She described where we were and I remembered a strange pause in the interaction. She told me that in that moment she wanted me to grab her tits and have my way with her.

I got the sense that this was a particular issue that had been ongoing over time and now that I write this I remember a time earlier in the relationship when I stayed over at her apartment. Maybe the second or third time I did so she wanted to rent a movie. At the movie-rental place she wanted to get a porn movie and I agreed. It turns out that it was an instructional video throughout which I couldn't help but laugh in my satirize-everything sort of way. I didn't get that night how disappointed she was that we didn't make love. She really did try a bunch of things to get me to open my desire nature to her and in retrospect I wish I hadn't caused her so much disappointment! She is a wonderful woman and I did desire her but I just couldn't open the gates to desire at that stage in my life. Her Mars-Mercury in Scorpio right on her Descendant are conjunct my Sun and so my presence stirred her own desire nature. She wanted to connect with me in ways I was not yet ready to experience. During the last bit of our time together we did manage to connect and have a sexual relationship in a way that seemed to work for both of us but I never really opened up to her in ways that would have reflected how I felt about her and the level of attraction I did have for her.

In my 30s when living in LA I dated a woman for a few months with a strong Leo signature who has an equally strong sex drive. But she also has Chiron in Aries in the 1st house and at that time was not yet processed on some difficult experiences in her sexual history. She had been molested as a child and in her adulthood had experienced

201

some difficult dynamics in a number of important relationships. I found her attractive and began to care for her but for the first few weeks we dated I didn't "make a move." She became certain that I wasn't attracted to her and this stirred up some of her experiences of feeling rejected and unloved that I perceived were related to some experiences with her Chiron in Aries/1st house. There was a time in my apartment when we were talking and making out and she brought it up. She told me she could tell that I wasn't attracted to her and nothing I would say would change her mind. In that state the wound came out and it wasn't a moment during which I felt like I wanted to share sexual intimacy. I wonder if I could have ripped off her clothes in that moment and gotten busy with her/got all up in her business if she would have believed that I found her attractive. But with that Chiron, other people's wounded states are not aphrodisiacs for me.

In the weeks prior, in the beginning of the getting-to-know-you phase, I had told her that when I was a kid I found anyone who had differently-colored skin fascinating. I grew up in a somewhat small town and was intrigued with people descended from people other than those from Northern Europe. It's a thing that can come with a stellium in Sagittarius – curiosity about and interest in diverse things and people from other places – and I told her as much. But on the night described above she latched on to this and decided that I was only attracted to women who weren't white. She decided that since she had blonde hair and blue eyes that this is why I didn't find her attractive. Nothing I could say for the duration of the relationship could shake that sure thought – that belief – out of her head. Most of the women I've dated happen to have blonde with blue eyes and so her idea was nonsense but it made sense to her given her need to find a reason that I was rejecting her by not sexualizing the relationship quickly. I told her that I move slowly and I don't think she had ever been around or with a man who did. After the relationship was over she told me that a major effect I had on her was loving her just as she was, that she knew she didn't have to do anything to get that love. But during the relationship this dynamic outlined quite the struggle.

As I write this I remember some experiences with my first girlfriend in college, my first sexual partner. I was slow then, too, as you can imagine given this karma of being afraid to do things to women for fear of doing something wrong. I remember a series of nights in the beginning of our time together holding hands, making out, and gazing into each other's eyes, sometimes staying up all night. She was extraordinarily patient with me for the 6 weeks or so that we dated before the end of the school year before she left town for the summer. I visited her at home for a week during that break and things did heat up but I didn't make the move to have sex with her. When she came back to school at the end of the Summer she took matters in her own hands, finally running out of patience and getting on top of me that first night back and taking me into her to relieve the tension that had been building for months. I was more or less disconnected from an

203

awareness of my body and many emotions during those years and so I just couldn't take the lead in that stage of my life.

Regarding this part of self, I have to acknowledge feeling memories of this other life while making choices grounded in the present. I am not the youth who stood by and watched a rape unfold. I am Tom Jacobs and can use that memory to inspire me to be present with women, which I do my best to do. A lot of these themes came up and I learned to work with and around them when I was with A. She was open to me and wanted to connect sexually with a lover. Her level of presence helped me learn to leave behind some of those fears of acting from desire. There was a particular night early in our dating when I knew she wanted me to bust out of whatever was holding me back and make a move, let the big cat inside me out of the cage. I saw myself clearly and felt the resistance and couldn't step out of it. The next time we saw each other, however, I did and she expressed a great deal of relief. She said she knew it was in there and had been trying to get to it, trying to give me space to let it come out.

It would be easy for me to be on edge regarding sexual violence and to begin to see it everywhere (even where it is not) but if I were to do that I would not be present. In my work I tend to draw people who've experienced their fair share of issues related to Venus-Pluto as well as Mars and Lilith. At times it does seem that I am surrounded by the results of sexual violence and I have to make sure I don't decide that this is what makes up the world. I would be reliving the past by carrying forward fear and an identity formed surrounded failing to do enough to protect a woman in trouble. The world is not full of wounded women. It is full of women in the process of learning how to be sexual beings as part of their path as divine beings learning about being human.

At this stage in my life I am navigating promoting self-published erotica.[15] It's been available for a while through the Kindle store but I haven't done anything to market it. It is satirical and, as such, healing for me – I satirize what I most need to heal. It is written from the male mindset that produces and consumes the majority of pornography while it satirizes the one-track mind and lower-chakra desires that can certainly be disconnected from the heart and spiritual centers. In a recent conversation with a colleague about my creative work, which I know with certainty needs to get more time and energy from me if I am to be truly happy, she asked me what would be true about me if that work were out there and I am known to have written it. I thought about it for a moment and realized that part of me thinks that I would be someone who doesn't love, cherish, respect, and nurture women. And that I would be someone who just takes advantage of women and uses them, treats them as objects for sexual gratification because that is the tenor of the narrators of the book. The women I've been with who enjoy sex want to some degree to be

[15] *Modern Love: Erotic Vignettes, Volume I.*

objectified – being found beautiful and attractive is a wonderful aphrodisiac. And you can't find anything about a person attractive without objectifying him or her – it's just how it works. It can be experienced as being celebrated as who you are and that has been part of my healing process given this other-life memory and how it has affected me as Tom Jacobs. One way to make sure I can balance this is to subjectify a woman as much as I objectify her. It leads to a good flow and, I admit, it's new for me.

This erotica is funny. No one who has read any bit of it or heard about it from me has not either laughed or split his or her side and seized from laughter. J. gets cramps in her middle from laughing at it and I've not heard her be laugh-triggered like that by anything else. My friends who know about it encourage me to get it out there because it's a healing tool and I'm slowly working toward that. It also seems to me many times that my metaphysical work might be or is more important than my creative work because of the healing potential, as mentioned in the previous chapter. It is true that parts of me do not want to be seen as someone who thinks in the way that the characters and narrators of that work do but, of course, they are parts of me and it's time that I own what is happening within them. I know I always have choice about how I live and behave.

Pluto-Venus conjunct in any sign indicate a deep need for intense sexual experience. Whether a person is conscious of this need and works toward creating experiences that serve it or is unconscious and bumbles around is another issue! The conjunction also says that deep levels of honesty are required for relationships to work. Boundaries are called for with this and there are times when a human with such a chart will not be intentional and conscious enough to know that before stepping out in one direction or another. The effect of offending or hurting another would then be deeply painful and could lead to the kind of hesitation I've experienced in this life as described above. This conjunction is in Libra and this adds to the story that there is a connection sought by this person. But if all cards are not on the table (important for anything in Libra but especially Pluto-Venus) then the person might not learn to be assertive in the right ways. In the 12th house there is a distinct risk that the chart holder might not be aware of his or her desires or needs or, even, expectations of others. All of it must come into conscious awareness and sometimes that happens through a process of trial and error in which some missteps are chosen or stumbled upon.

The opposition to Chiron-Eris in Aries in the 7th house deepens the story. Any unconscious Pluto-Venus behavior (because they are in the 12th house) can lead to confronting and being confronted by others' wounds and insecurities. In many lives I probably draw to me people with hot buttons and difficulties regarding sex and then take reflection from them that I'm doing something wrong and, in turn, develop my own complexes about it. As acknowledged above it can be that uninformed and less-than-conscious choices can be made too but there is also the possibility that I take too much meaning from the responses of others who have difficulties regarding sex and then I also have difficulties regarding sex even if I did not before the interactions. This chart set up says that I will draw such people to me until I choose to stop it through altering how I select others to be in relationship with and learning to say "no" when encountering people who might not know how to work through their difficult issues carried forward from the past. The metaphysical truth is that it's only in my sphere because I am still willing to experience it.

Mars and Uranus together bring an erratic experience of sexual energy and, at times, potentially a disconnection from it and all physicality in general. Uranus is about inventiveness, individuality, and originality but it also relates to the ability to be objective to the point of being stuck in one's head and losing identification with the body. In the 1st house I carry the two energies in my physical body strongly. At times I have walked up to a woman with nothing particular on my mind and had her recoil because of my strong energy field. In fact, one woman with whom I had occasional contact as a colleague at a workplace in LA shrank back from me when she first encountered me. She turned the corner into the opening to my cubicle and clearly regretted it, also clearly not knowing how to remove herself gracefully. I was surprised and felt into her reaction as she stumbled through delivering what she had come to say. The energy was something close to if not,

"You remind me of my rapist." At the time I was in danger of developing a bit of a malfunction about such things but now I get that something in my field made her uncomfortable. Who knows – maybe I know her in another life and she was someone with whom I made a misstep. It's also entirely possible it was just that she found herself uncomfortable around me for her own reasons that had nothing to do with me. I know that as Tom Jacobs I'm more responsible for my energy than in some others and that I've erred on the side of withholding sharing it with others, to the chagrin of a girlfriend here and there.

A Military Officer

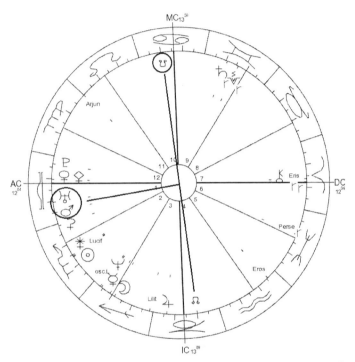

Covered in this chapter: SN in the 10th, Mars-Uranus in the 1st square the nodes.

The first major integration that took place after my move to Tucson in 2009 was the result of an intentional fragment retrieval I performed on myself. Ascended Master Djehuty had taught me a process similar in some ways to soul retrieval facilitated by shamans in traditional cultures all over the globe. He encouraged me to teach it to others to use on themselves and I have been doing that for several years with great results. It differs from the traditional approach in that one does not need an intermediary. Also, instead of a journey one contacts fragments lost or elsewhere on the timeline in a unique way that creates an emotional bridge that can lead to conscious integration of the fragment or other-life persona.

I always have a specific purpose in mind when I do it, as Djehuty instructs. Running my business and being my own everything specialist arose from necessity and I was feeling challenged by the marketing bit in addition to everything else. The logistics of employing someone else never seemed right and so I decided to call forward a me from another life who could help me with my marketing process. I went through the meditative process to call the persona in and within a day or so I had access to this other portion of consciousness.

When one does this process the need of the moment is what determines what part of self or other-life parallel returns or makes contact. Therefore I had no idea that I would get a sort of drill sergeant intent on whipping my entire life into shape! At first it was strange because I could tell he was from another century. He felt mid to late 19th century and Northern European. In time I narrowed it down to Prussia and the military through a process of asking questions and feeling into the answers.

His earliest contribution had to do with trying to get me to go to the gym every day. He decided that I was much too overweight and that was the first thing that had to be changed. How I experienced this was via thoughts when I would catch a glimpse of myself in a mirror or notice how my clothes fit and what it was like to move my body. There was a new urgency to make a change. I let him know that my norm of 3 times each week at the gym was sufficient, attempting to establish for him that I would continue being the one to make decisions in my life.

After a few days I got used to the feeling of being more energized and optimistic. He brought a can-do attitude and that was just what I needed to get the marketing bit organized and furthered. I saw that I had more work ahead of me – a bunch of things I had not wanted to do before – but felt better about tackling it. With a SN in the 10th house in certain lives I've been conditioned by living in environments that instill a can-do attitude. Life in the 10th house can be focused on accomplishment and success but also developing competency in order for a skill and/or quality of character to be recognized by others. This officer's at-the-ready stance reflects a military philosophy of life in which one never knows what will be needed and so it's best to be prepared for anything.

It's true that 10th-house ways of life involve being seen or regarded by a community in one way or another. Life here also involves becoming a symbol to others of what you do in the world. This man's identification with his life as a soldier runs deep and in fact parallels other parts of me that are prone to identify with my work. Often I have to ensure I detach from the flow of work that seems to want to come and be articulated through me. I have to in order to feel that I have a full life, a normal issue with a 10th-house SN. The NN in the 4th calls for developing inner awareness and knowing what makes one tick. It calls for stepping back from 10th house activities and emphases including work.

This part of self from another life also relates to Mars conjunct Uranus in the 1st house and square the nodal axis. The right use of will, self-assertion, freedom, and individuality need to be learned by Tom Jacobs. We can know that what comes with the two planets square the nodes will involve some trial and error. If I tend toward being timid then I need to step out and be more visible and obviously energetic. If I tend toward being out there most of the time then I need to learn to check my energy and behavior in order to learn to inhabit the middle ground. No extreme will do with a square to the nodes but exploring extremes is part and parcel of the learning journey. The military officer tends toward a robust expression of these physical energies and, in fact, doesn't want to slow down unless it's absolutely necessary. I have tended toward trying to keep some of my energy on the down-low so I don't stand out too much for the wrong reasons – an adaptation to trial-and-error situations about which I haven't felt good– and so have needed to step out with more confidence and self-assertion.

There were minor things I needed to integrate and instruct him regarding such as certain social realities in the year 2011. In line at a local coffee shop I found myself confused and extremely uncomfortable that there was a person in line ahead of me with brown skin. I realized that in the military officer's space-time location his surroundings are pretty homogenous. Northern Europe in the mid-19th century would not have had many people with brown skin out and about in shops. I wondered if he had even ever seen a person with African ancestry. I explained to him (by talking to myself in my head) that in the year 2011 in the USA there are people running around with all possible skin colors and, in fact, many shades between as a result of mixed heritages. I told him this was perfectly normal given my social context and that he needed to get used to it. He more or less did but now and again I do feel this part of my consciousness a bit resistant to being surrounded by people who don't appear to have purely Northern European ancestry. This doesn't make him a bigot as much as it tells of the narrow and limited context in which that human lives in his spot on the Earth timeline – it's counter to what he expects, his comfort zone. That I don't hate myself (or him) for experiencing that attitude does not make me a bigot either. It means that I'm multidimensional and there are parts of me living on other spots of the Earth timeline that bleed through occasionally who don't find my social context immediately comfortable.

This is a great example of looking at how we usually identify with our emotions. If a person who is otherwise egalitarian had the feeling of discomfort around someone with different skin color (and didn't deny or stuff the feeling), wouldn't it be normal for him or her to wonder even if for just a brief moment if he or she is racist or a bigot? Our minds are wonderful at doubting how great we think we are! It seems to me that it would be entirely normal but the model of what it means to be human that I'm offering you in these pages is meant to open you to seeing things in a new way. Given this model it's true that a part of me has opinions based in his timeline context that would look to Tom Jacobs as fitting with bigotry or racism but this does not make me (or him) a racist. *This model of what it means to be human asks us to conceive of ourselves in a new way that allows complexity of internal opinions, beliefs, attitudes, and thoughts while it invites us to cease judging what we find within us.* At the same time it invites us to make decisions about what versions of ourselves we wish to invest in given that there are so many possibilities with the complexities of our energetic and emotional signatures. As I teach people to integrate other-life parts as described in these pages I emphasize getting grounded and staying in the body and regularly clearing out the mind and energy field. It is critical to have a baseline sense of self before doing this work and maintaining and reinforcing that baseline while doing it.

By explaining my social context to this part of my consciousness that was bleeding through I was asserting that I know who I am as Tom Jacobs and the bleed through's ideas were not going to overpower mine. This was one instance of what amounts to orientation and coaching of the bleed through so it can learn to be present within the field of consciousness without being given permission to dominate and take over. I didn't flinch because of this other-life man's feelings or look at the brown person in a funny or disapproving way. I stood in line and waited my turn, doing nothing this part of me might have done because of his inexperience and ignorance due to a lack of experience with varied skin tones.

A Cancer SN can describe a multilife journey of being surrounded in many lives by those in most ways like you. This is the sign of community and nation but also family and clan. It's about relating to life through the lens of belonging and acceptance. Homogeneity chosen by a community or clan is one way of protecting the group. *Limiting outside influences can keep the blood and community lines pure* is how the thinking usually goes. At times this can lead to a distrust of people who are different. When we learn over the course of many lives through the sign associated with the Moon we learn that we need to stick together. This can of course have people fearing what is different and trying to maintain it and others who bring that energy out of our spheres. So it is natural that this military office in his Northern European context would get nervous being around people with different skin colors.

The other thing to note with this particular man is that once I had become comfortable with his go-getter attitude and was appreciating that he returned, I woke up one day and felt the urge to shave off my goatee. It wasn't out of character for me to suddenly change my mind about something like that so I didn't think twice. I expected nothing out of the ordinary but once it was gone I looked in the mirror and saw that I had the beginning of a double chin! The military officer came forward and said something like, "See what I mean?! You have to go to the gym more like I told you!" I (he) had this righteous feeling that he'd been proven right – and I'd been tricked. Every time I looked in the mirror after that until I grew it back I was reminded that he thought I needed to lose some weight.

I had to laugh because it was indeed clever. But I took it as a cue that when other-life parts bleed through and/or return they not only bring the skills you might have been lacking that precipitated their return or your invitation to come back but they also bring a will and ideas of their own. Now, around two years after calling him back he still has some judgments about my weight but I let him know I'm fine with how I am and I put him to work on the marketing tasks. He loves being creative and active to do those things and that makes the recall and integration a success as far as I'm concerned.

This man's ability to see things in black and white can be a hindrance and I often have to check my reactions to certain situations. A positive side of this is that I can't hem and haw when it comes to a goal – it either is to happen or it isn't. A negative is that if I let him take over fully for a day or part of one, I don't enjoy it at all! Tempering his influence while being grateful for it is the key. He is inclined not to stop until all the jobs are done. But the thing is that my job as a marketer of my work never ends and so I have to call it a day when I am ready to do and be more than a one-track-minded go-getter.

A Patriarchal Man

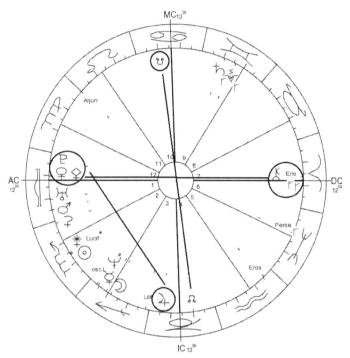

Covered in this chapter: SN in Cancer/10ᵗʰ, Pluto-Venus-Pallas Athene in Libra/12ᵗʰ square Jupiter in Capricorn/3ʳᵈ, Venus-Pallas Athene square the nodes, Chiron-Eris in Aries/7ᵗʰ square the nodes.

When J. and I went to Yakima for the intensive in September of 2011 I learned about another life that deserves mention. As Tom Jacobs I'm heavily Libran and fairness seems to be extremely important. At the workshop I found myself getting to know a part of self who isn't so much interested in fairness as having others do things that he would prefer they do. This part of self is clear that things are easier if one person in the room is making the decisions. (Easier for whom, you ask? Him, of course!) In the process of feeling that conditioned desire I was able to avoid expressing what it would have had me do in favor of how I wanted to behave. It one was one of the few times living through an other-life story in which I was not taken over by an emotion or belief but observed it and interacted with the persona while I made my own choices.

The woman who organized and hosted the workshop had been a client for a couple of years and we had become friendly. Prior to and during this trip as we worked out business decisions related to producing the workshop I tapped into memories from a life in which I had been a strong-willed male and she had been a less than strong-willed female. I don't know precisely what the dynamic in that other life is but I sense they might be spouses.

Now, patriarch is not a bad word. Patriarchy is not the end of the world, a prison sentence, or the equivalent to a four-letter word. It is simply one way of organizing life, the world, and self and other. The kind of imbalanced social order we live with and through that we term patriarchy arises when the energy of the masculine is in any way elevated over that of the feminine.[16] But how we have done it has not simply been to shift the balance in one direction for a while or for certain ways of living. We have in fact attempted to tie down and shame what resists control and domination, which is to say the natural feminine in just about all of its forms. This person living elsewhere on the Earth timeline I found myself tapping into is not a bad man but is one who inhabits the masculine ideal of his time and expects women to inhabit the counterbalancing, prevalent ideal of the feminine of the time. This has been going on for around 6,000 years in a number of cultures on Earth and all humans have at least at some time from either side of the gender line done what they could to fit in to the cultural agenda, following instructions regarding how men and women are supposed to conceive of themselves, be, and treat each other.

In this part of my consciousness I see this pattern and relate it in part to Pluto-Venus issues because they can cause a person come to believe that power must be gained and held over a partner. It's an ugly expression of the two energies but is certainly one possibility when the planet of (trying to figure out how to have) power meets the planet of (trying to figure out how to have) relationship. The square from the conjunction to Jupiter in Capricorn/3rd can lead to beliefs becoming entrenched in the mind that don't work well and that bring friction to how relationships are

---

[16] See the books *Living Myth: Exploring Archetypal Journeys*, *Goddess Past, Present, and Future* and *Lilith: Healing the Wild* for explorations of and remedies for this situation.

actually working (square Venus). Ideas and thought patterns about controlling others is one potential result.

I also see Chiron-Eris in Aries on the Descendant implicated here. They are square the nodal axis, indicating that fairness and forthrightness in relationship are issues that need to be resolved. If a wound exists with the Chiron energy here then when it comes to the surface the chaos and competition of Eris can come with it. It might be expected that in some people at least some of the time this sort of signature could result in taking an Aries stance within relationship that does not flow freely with the normal and natural give and take that enable healthy relationships to form, grow, and thrive. It may at times seem as if a rigid Aries/7th house position is needed in order to protect the natural vulnerabilities of the self with partnership (Chiron in Aries/7th). These bodies also oppose Venus in Libra/12th and such a position might serve to try to have some semblance of self control within relationship that in fact becomes control of others.

The Cancer SN in the 10th house has to do with absorbing social, cultural, and tribal conditioning. While the total of our many lives does not fit within the last 6,000 years during which patriarchal thought has flourished on the planet, each of us does have a fair amount of lives that take place during that time. Since we are coming out of those ways of being now it makes sense that our tribal and cultural issues from the last few thousand years would be ripe to come to the surface now. There are echoes everywhere of old ways of being when it comes to how to behave as a woman or a man. My SN in the sign of tradition (Cancer) in the house of society (10th) represents a number of lives on the planet in which I let myself be defined by cultural and tribal expectations. Even without reports from me about what's unfolding in my awareness of my soul's other lives it would be safe to assume that my soul is erupted into spots along the timeline where its humans are drinking in and espousing cultural values when it comes to how men and women are supposed to be. In my present life in many arenas I am acutely aware of what society expects and seems to require. Uranus in the 1st house often takes over with the energy of rebellion and I don't comply with those expectations and requirements but I have an awareness nonetheless.

The woman who organized the workshop and I had worked together to create the event – a very Libran sort of thing in some ways. She was in the process of learning to stand up on her own two feet and ask for what she wants and needs, which was a process of giving herself permission to have opinions, desires, and needs and, therefore self-respect. At several points as we worked out financial and logistical details for the weekend I had the sense that the way we were interacting in this life might be brand new between us across time. I could see clearly that she was trying out on me how much respect and validation I was willing to give her. Memories of not ever really hearing her speak about anything – including thoughts and opinions – surfaced within me. I'm not sure from where in me this comes but when others wait for me to treat them with respect or validate them so they can have permission to do it for themselves I challenge them to do it for themselves. I sense burrs under my saddle when others wait for or expect me to give them permission to be strong and confident. In my work I'm constantly sharing tools and tricks to help people see how to give them permission to be strong and I can't do the opposite in my personal life. It will not, after all, do to have one Divine being giving another permission to be confident! It doesn't work that way. Coming out of Piscean Age ways of thinking and into Aquarian Age ways, we simply must grasp that we are in charge of ourselves and, in fact, always have been. Our beliefs and choices determine the world we create around us. I respect myself and I respect your right to choose to respect yourself or put it off and wait for someone else to give you permission but that person will not be me.

As I listened to her in the planning phase and then weeks later during the intensive itself as she participated I felt a hint of a pull from habit not to encourage her to speak; to avoid holding space for her to express herself. I am not entirely sure what is going on in other lives when we know each other but it feels to me it could be a marriage in which I as the patriarchal man am ensuring that my wife is living up to the patriarchal expectations of a married woman. I can feel now that on that part of the timeline it feels good to have control and a sense of power but it also feels lonely! Don't assume that all those men across time who have been trained to treat women as somehow not as important or worthy as men always get off on it. Living life with someone who is kept small because of these cultural and religious teachings is pretty boring when it comes down to it. You have to become so full of yourself that you don't even notice that other people (women) are more than functions of the environment you've designed and set in motion or objects to perform certain tasks. The cost of that dominance is being surrounded by people are not perceived by others and may not perceive themselves to be equals in any way.

This brings to mind a note I find interesting and that I explored in *Lilith: Healing the Wild*. It is that the patriarchal mindset and its efficient vehicles – monotheistic religions that seed culture and society – each have a strict code that it is necessary or God's will or whatever that holds that men are to respect women. When I've explained the Lilith story to clients over the years including the notes on controlling and dominating the natural feminine to the point of being unable and unwilling to respect it, some clients have insisted that the religion in which they were raised or are emotionally or spiritually attached to now has clear requirements that women be respected. I have pointed out to them that this is true but that there are rules: women are respected only if they comport themselves according to the male/masculine/monotheistic religious ideal of what a women should be and do. The woman will get tons of respect and adulation for fulfilling the masculine mind's idea of what a woman is, yes, and this is great if it's all you can see and you want to fit in to a world in which a man's idea is held above all else. But it stinks if you can't deny your changing, cyclic, emotional, receptive, soft, flowing – *feminine* – nature. It is horrible if you trust your body and its wisdom and natural cycles but are expected to vilify and shame them in order to fit in and be acceptable. It is absolutely no fun if you happen to have deep-seated convictions that go against the patriarchal grain. Respecting women if they fulfill a masculine-prescribed ideal while failing to honor the natural feminine in all its forms is not respecting women but glorifying the masculine ideal of the feminine as it has developed over the last 6,000 years of life on Earth.

During the two days of the workshop I found myself curious at times to know what the woman was thinking. She generously chimed in to comment on the charts and lives of the other 6 attendees and asked a fair number of questions. She had learned a lot from me before this in readings and coaching and had shared numerous insights into how I see and do astrology. It was exciting to me to hear her thoughts and ideas and along the way I worked with a memory of being less than happy somewhere else on the timeline. That experience seems to me now like a balancing of something left unfinished in other lives.

Venus-Pallas Athene in Libra and square the nodes opposing Chiron-Eris in Aries/7th point out imbalance when it comes to relationship. The basic currency of relating is communication. The opportunity to correct an imbalance was becoming apparent as I found myself eager to hear what the woman might have to say about the material of and her experience attending the workshop. To heal this opposition square the nodes on the self-other angle (Ascendant-Descendant) requires listening more if you're inclined to avoid it, speaking up more if that's what you're inclined not to do, and in general showing up as someone available to find out what it takes and how to work to create equality with others. In each case relationship is an ongoing process of working to achieve balance between two people. We don't always see this (and this is why our relationships unfold, crash, and burn as they often can!) but it is how it works. Imbalances of many different kinds result and correcting them requires coming back to find middle ground with others.

There are times when I expect the committee process of waiting for others to weigh in to be draining. This part of me is clear that one person making the decisions is easier and better because it is faster and more efficient. My awareness of those feelings and beliefs gives me the opportunity to slow down enough to let the other speak. As described above, when I did that in this case I found myself interested in what the other has to say and following through with this way of being makes my Pluto-Venus feel that I'm on track because progress with others can be had. I don't often find that work unpleasant but there are parts of my consciousness on other parts of the Earth timeline that would. As mentioned elsewhere in this book, I make the decision that I'm in charge of the Tom Jacobs experience and, as soon as I see what's happening and begin to shift it, karmic bleed throughs don't run the show.

A Woman Who Lost Her Mind

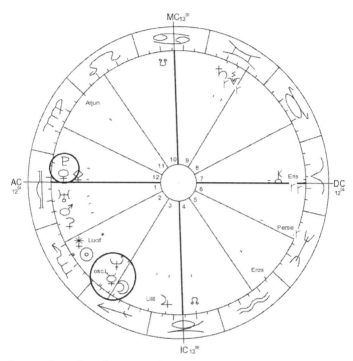

Covered in this chapter: Pluto-Venus in the 12th house, SN ruler conjunct Lilith-Neptune-Mercury in Sagittarius.

After the experiences that you've read about in this book it should come as no surprise that when this part surfaced, I knew what was happening, what to do to stay aware of myself, and how keep living my own life. I should say that of all the lives represented in these pages this one was and is the most frightening to deal with. Because I am more or less intentional about how my process will unfold (I state that it will be as gentle as possible and I will be invited to work with only what I can handle, preventing overwhelm) I know that when it came to the surface it was the first time I'd be able to deal with meeting this part of consciousness.

One night I was brushing my teeth before going to bed and had a flash dissociation from myself. These are not uncommon – momentary blips of bleed-throughs and memories from other parts of the timeline – but this one didn't end right away. I had the experience of knowing who Tom Jacobs is and yet that me felt foreign. It was just a few seconds of this before I realized that a part from another life had bled through or was returning after fragmentation. I paused before going to the bedroom but knew I needed some support and proceeded. J. was transiting out of the day, too, and I got in bed beside her. I was afraid to talk or look at her directly but I did take her hand after a few minutes. She was doing something on her computer and didn't notice anything strange with me being still next to her until I reached out.

Somehow I did tell her after a few minutes that something was happening. She spent the next 40 or so minutes staying present with me as I articulated the feelings, processed them, and worked to calm the part of consciousness that had just surfaced.

The sound of my voice frightened this returned part of me as it did not recognize the sound. The voice was weird enough for it but my hands almost drove this part over the edge! I observed that my hands seemed big and square, like paddles. Like big workman's hands but I wasn't a workman - that just didn't feel true. I kept looking at them as I talked with J. and I realized that this part I was dealing with is a woman. Even as this other-life part of self was on the verge of panic I stayed grounded and calm as much as I could while feeling that I was two people who shouldn't be in the same body.

After touching my hands and J.'s hands and face, and J. touching parts of me at my request, I felt this woman within me edging toward panic even more. She seemed perpetually on the verge of losing control of herself and diving in to hysterics. I had to do the affirmation, "I am always safe, I am always secure" many times over the following 40 minutes to keep all of me calm. It seemed that her response to everything was to rush to panic so I felt into things a bit deeper, even as I was managing her multiple layers of fear and my discomfort.

I had the sense that she is clear that she has lost her mind. I've seen this as a potential with soul journeys featuring Pluto in the 12th house and other Neptunian signatures but hadn't felt that it was true for me outside the other-life drug use and botched consciousness-expansion attempts alluded to in an earlier chapter. Simply feeling insane or perceiving that I was losing or had lost my mind had not seemed a part of my multilife experience before that night.

I continually reinforced the energetic cords I had into the Earth and repeated the affirmation, "I am always safe, I am always secure." I remembered that a few weeks earlier I had told members at a meeting of the Tucson Astrologers' Guild to whom I was giving a talk on 2012/the End of the Mayan Calendar that deep down I had a fear of losing my mind. It was in the context of Plutonian fears in each of the houses while mentioning my Pluto in the 12th. I said that in other lives maybe this has happened to me and that's why I didn't want to channel or be a medium in this life – perhaps I didn't want to feel out of control of myself and my mind. During the talk I remarked to myself – observing me giving the talk, which is a common experience I have during talks and classes – that I had never really thought of that before and that it was interesting. I wondered what was going to come up now that the thought had crossed my mind!

With J. next to me and meeting my gaze as much as I could handle I slowly calmed down. She was rock solid and I felt so grateful for her support. For most of those 40 or so minutes I felt on the edge of panic-induced asthma, which I had experienced several times since 2009. It seems that since then I learned numerous ways to overstimulate the liver to dump energy way too quickly, with one result being that excess energy rushes from the liver to the lungs[17] with the result of panicky asthma. I knew that the

---

[17] I am told by people in the know about meridians that there is no direct link between these two lines but that this effect can happen nonetheless.

mullein tincture in the next room would help because it relaxes the mucous membranes in the respiratory tract but I also knew that it would have to be fetched. I felt clear that I needed to do it myself and not ask J. to get it for me. It took a couple of minutes of extreme focus to get grounded enough to get up and stand on and use my feet but I did it. I took the mullein though I felt with some confidence that I could continue calming this part of self and keep staving off panic. My thought was that it was possible for this part of self to remain afraid and in attempts to communicate with me as I slept wake me up in full panic mode. This happened one of the first times I had the panicky asthma a couple of years prior and if I can avoid waking up in a full-bore panic state again, I will.

From J.'s perspective it was as though I was having a bad drug trip and we laughed about it even as it was happening. Each of us has had our share of altered states from adventures in consciousness and when I have support and someone who can help me stay grounded it's fun to share it. I was fully aware of this other-life woman's feelings and fears while I remembered all I know about other-life parts, getting grounded, and integrating them. This woman inside me offered me the image that people in clinical positions were telling her and saying about her that she was insane and that she had lost her mind. I could tell that she was in an institution of some kind that it was not during a part of the timeline in which psychology or psychiatry are what they are today. I have the sense that she is in a place in which people whom clinicians don't know what to do with are placed to keep out of the way of all the normal people. It reminded me that there are numbers of people diagnosed as mentally ill who are in fact having multidimensional consciousness experiences that no one – including them – understands. I shared this with the other-life part and reassured her that she is not and I am not crazy but there are some difficult experiences and emotions to deal with. I let her see that I'm skilled in these things and am committed to keeping my head screwed on straight. I helped her to feel safe being part of me and in a bit I/we felt much better. I was able to sleep after a while without incident, feeling deep relief that I was able to stay this side of panic. It was perhaps the most intense altered-consciousness state I'd had.

A few days later J. and I were watching a documentary that included a discussion about a lack of human empathy on the planet being a source of our collective problems. An image from an art or sciencey-type film that was aimed at evoking an empathetic response was included depicting a graphic, violent act. An attractive brunette woman sitting in a chair was smiling at the camera. Someone standing behind her opened a straight razor and sliced into her left eye. I screamed and ran out of the room, seized with fear.

My whole life I've had an issue with violent images and not being about to get them out of my mind but this was the worst of all. I went to the living room and sat with my arms crossed, trying not to scream bloody murder from my anger at having been surprised with that footage. J.

turned it off and I could see she was affected, too. We talked about it briefly but I was in no shape to calm down or be reasonable. After a couple of hours I was able to come out of it but the image was still in my mind and it bothered me deeply. Then a few hours later I was going to sleep and appeared to have all but forgotten about the incident but the image flashed in my mind as I began to drift off. I woke with a start and realized this part that had returned the previous week was panicking. Having a horrific image playing in her mind was about the worst thing she could imagine. To her that is a symbol of having lost her mind because she can't keep out the unwanted thoughts and images that, presumably, eventually consume one. Repetitive and obsessive thoughts from which she cannot escape seem to typify at least part of her situation.

I went to the living room with my laptop to watch a movie for a bit. Each time I got really tired and closed my eyes the panic was there. Twice I shut down my computer and attempted to bed down on the couch and each time I all but freaked out when I closed my eyes. I did sleep eventually but I think it was around 2-3 hours in total. J. came out the next morning to say goodbye as she went to work and I could tell she could see I was in and had been in a state. For the next few hours I tried to keep calm but my attitude was awful because of the lack of sleep. Optimism and calm are the first things to go when I'm sleep-deprived.

Around mid-day I decided to get more grounded than I had been that week, willing myself to bring calm and confidence back. The human strength of will is amazing – we can be stuck in a state of despair or anything else and make the decision to step out of it. It's something I teach my coaching clients and students but to do it requires some time of practice voluntarily entering and exiting challenging emotional states. Djehuty often asks people he works with to make a firm decision from a grounded state and perhaps he reminded me that this was an option for me. Either way, I felt inspired to get back on track as me and smooth out this part's panic while ridding myself of the image or adapting to it.

Once I willed myself back to a grounded state I saw the truth that I couldn't get the image out of my mind – you can't unsee something and if it had an impact you maybe shouldn't hope to forget it. I stayed in my body and decided that I was always safe and secure and I let the image come up and play in my mind. I gently but firmly instructed myself that all was fine and I was safe and secure. The image made me flinch as it had the night prior and I replayed it until I no longer flinched or reacted. This is to say that I did the affirmation alongside the image until this part of me recently returned was calm enough not to fear or hate the image. I calmed this part of self by providing a deep level of confidence that even though we had seen that awful image and it was still in my head, everything was fine and that this part is safe. She calmed down and I knew from my work doing this with clients that this is an indicator that she had come to trust me. She was able to see that my tools, skills, understanding, and confidence are enough to create the feeling of safety that she never had and had been lacking since she returned to me. I had been somewhat grounded and together but as I dealt with her fears for almost a week in the process of calming her, I had not felt confident, firm, and clear that all was and would continue to be fine. I had been refeeling aspects of her life and trying to talk her down, which took a lot of energy and it was now time to focus on me as the decision-maker in my life and the one in charge. My efforts had been working but from time she returned to this moment I had not fully inhabited my consciousness sorcerer, other-life journeying, multidimensional self. That side of me is what I bring into readings for others but what I had been going through during the week had been taking my attention and I didn't think of it until I did. It was all for the best, though, because it has proved important that I know more about this returned woman who was sure she has lost her mind. I am better able to deal with her on a daily basis now because of the insights gained during that week.

Once I was comfortable with the image replaying in my mind and she was comfortable and not freaking out or on the verge of panic, it was about 2 minutes until I began writing this book. I was sitting on the couch in the living room, J. having left several hours earlier for work. I thought I was going to write about that particular process and what I had experienced and learned and then began typing out the introductory material that became this volume. It didn't even seem to matter that I was so low on sleep and had been all over the map emotionally – the words began to pour out in more or less the right order. The experience with the other-life woman had enabled me to put enough twos with other twos that it was finally time for me to begin articulating all the fours of these processes.

Astrologically, the SN ruler conjunct Neptune indicates that in my human lives I keep showing up as a Neptunian figure in all the ways that this implies. Dreamy, mystical, escapist, creative, deceptive, inspired, addictive, lost, in tune with the divine – all of it is possible among the many chapters of human lives my soul is living along the Earth timeline. SN ruler Moon is also conjunct the true Black Moon Lilith, which brings in the notion of changeable, erratic swings.[18] We might think Moon is about that kind of swings and it is but with Lilith conjunct it there is a definite edge of the wild being carried by these other-life mes and the one named Tom Jacobs. The wild when it comes to Lilith has to do with being connected to the wisdom of nature carried in our lower chakras. It is instinctive guidance that many of us mostly do what we can to train ourselves out of knowing and trusting. The pull of the natural world when existing in our bodies can have us moving in directions that our minds are afraid to approach. One word that is appropriate here that goes with Lilith is "unpredictable." What I get about myself as Tom Jacobs is that I have spent a great deal of time controlling my mind so that I can ensure that I do not

---

[18] See *Lilith: Healing the Wild.*

suffer because of what can happen when one does not control it. Now with this particular part returned and integrated I can see what the feared danger is. I understand more about my strategies to stay in control of my mind and all that enters, leaves, and unfolds within it so that I don't have to deal with the possibility that I might lose my mind.

As a channel and medium I have experience working my mind in tandem with energies and levels of consciousness that are not rooted in time-space. I've channeled ascended masters, interfaced with spirit guides of all kinds, met (and had my mind blown by) an angel, and conversed with and channeled an alien intelligence and have come out of all those experiences without any scratches or dents. But as a person I can see that I carry fears about bringing insanity into the world and being seen as someone who doesn't know how to live in it. As I write this I am tapping into the fact that when your mind is going off in an odd direction and you are losing the ability to function in society and life, it is often true that others can see it before you can. At least, I should say, this is the fear that comes to the surface. My work as a channel and medium prove to me that lots of varying styles of being and levels of consciousness can be factored into a healthy human life – it doesn't have to be about totalitarian control of mind or an utter lack of sanity. It's not that simple and the false dichotomy should not be feared. It needs to be dismantled so that I can be present to how it's best for me to be in a given moment.

The trick with Lilith is to be willing to flow with the needs and desires of the moment. As an instinctive energy it represents a level of intelligence that connects us to our biology in a simple but profound way. When we rely on instinct we find our bodies and internal chemical factories communicating with us constantly. If we can come to trust them then we position ourselves to accept our animal natures even as we manage all levels of our being, not just favor the mind and deny the rest with occasional necessary body maintenance. In this life I seem to be getting great insights through intuition, guidance, and experience that show me how to use this Lilith to my advantage instead of feeling used by it. When I flow with it I am better able to manage my Neptune energy, as well, which by extension leaves me willing and open to explore my Pluto in the 12th house, that most important placement when it comes to connecting with and honoring the soul's journey.

A Spartan

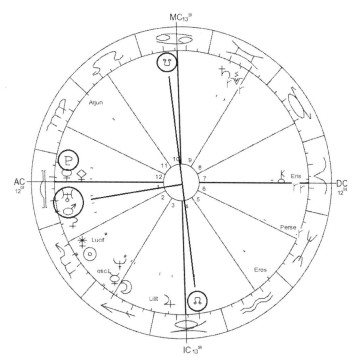

Covered in this chapter: Pluto in the 12th, SN in Cancer/10th and NN in Capricorn/4th, Mars-Uranus in the 1st square the nodes.

When I began broadcasting my radio show The Soul's Journey in October 2012 I was contacted by a woman offering to be a guest on the show. She reads Akashic records and it seemed to her that my show might be a good fit given its emphasis on soul, its multilife journey, and healing and release. I asked if she would like to do a trade so we can sample each other's work before we went on the air. She agreed and as of this writing, yesterday I had my reading with her.

I went into the reading seeking support and shifting regarding anger. Elsewhere in this book you've read that this has been an issue in my life. I've sought various routes to working with it and thought I'd try this woman's work with the records. I thought that if I could identify an other-life source, a particular event, then I would be able to release the source of the anger. Her work includes clearing energies, too, so I was looking forward to the possibilities.

Toward the beginning of the discussion she discerned that there were more selves in my field than just me. She said I was carrying two additional portions of consciousness and that it would be good for them to go. One was an entity I had taken on from my (somewhat depressive) father when I was a kid. The other was a warrior who presented with an extreme level of reactivity and from what she could see was a source of my experience of anger now. She opened the records and saw that this was a person with whom I was connected as a soldier in a life in the Greek region of Sparta around 500 B.C.E. The two of us shared a brotherly bond but were not related by blood. There was an oath between the two men to protect and save each other if possible, which certainly would come in handy with brothers in arms on the battlefield.

In my present life at age 8 I had a respiratory infection and my mom took my to our pediatrician's office. I was seen by the nurse, a dreary, drab older lady with zero ability to comfort or nurture a child. When the needle she was intending to use came out I mustered the courage to tell her that I was terrified and that I needed her to tell me everything she was going to do before she did it. She looked me in the eye, seeming to take me seriously, and said, "Yes, of course, I will do that for you. I will tell you everything—" and then suddenly stabbed my thigh with the needle, intentionally disregarding my request. I'm sure she thought of me as just another annoying kid making her life a drag and that she knew how they needed be treated no matter what they said.

I screamed from panic and we ran out of the office. My leg had seized when she stabbed me and it was completely stiff. My mom kind of lead-dragged me out to the car, very upset. I was in shock and I felt angry but that I couldn't do anything about any of it. We drove home and my mom apologized numerous times for what had happened, though of course it was not at all her fault. I think she felt and might to this day feel a bit like she should have been able to protect me. Since then I've had issues with medical personnel getting near me with needles and sharps of all kinds and when I went through a period in my 20s when a series of nurses, GPs, and phlebotomists had problems locating veins when attempting to draw blood, I shriveled up in terror and felt traumatized. They would stick the needle into my arm and fish around for a vein. I've attributed this to other-life selves elsewhere on the Earth timeline undergoing torture but it's been too intense to get into before very recently. Locating the root of torture in my other lives was part of my intention for this Akashic records reading – because I figured it was a source of anger – though we didn't quite get there that day when all was said and done.

The reader told me that when that stabbing happened this warrior brother from the life in ancient Sparta returned to protect me. The contract to protect each other was still in play and a door opened. Just after the event at age 8 I was in shock but I do remember a few of the disoriented minutes of the car ride back home. I remember my mom's regret and anger, her apologies to me that this had happened. She was angry enough for the both of us! We didn't go back to that office and I transitioned into seeing a GP from then on.

What came out in the reading recently was that I have been dealing with this other man's aggressive tactics to try to protect me. From what I can sense, his reactions are out of context to whatever is in front of me – they are too extreme. I have sought to create a gentle expression of self in this life that feels right and gets closer to what I see as a Pluto-in-Libra ideal of peace, harmony, and justice, but I have been juggling that with the extreme reactions of this Spartan warrior who is determined not to allow anything to hurt me. It's intense and has taken a tremendous amount of energy to try to become calm these last 32 years. When I have a sense of peace within me it often happens that something small happens and I react out of all proportion. I attribute this to having the energy of a highly-trained but highly-reactive warrior inside my field with me. He's been angry that I was hurt and my normal experience the last 3+ decades has been feeling his anger! No wonder I've been so reactive.

Yet the real point of this chapter is not this entity that was cleared, this brother in arms who rushed in to save my child self when I had been violated. In the hours following the reading I explored a new sense of calm, which I had expected because when others are cleared from your field you will feel more whole and less diluted or commixed. My work often creates this effect within clients but it's rare that I've experienced it to the same degree myself from a reading with a human. For me it typically happens when working with guides and masters.

During this calm that came to the surface later in the day, the other-life Spartan that is associated with my soul became apparent. I felt the signature of a calm, clear-headed warrior with much training who could think solidly on his feet no matter what was unfolding around him. As I connected with him I felt that everything was simple and straightforward and that little warranted reaction. Sometimes when at home and being forgetful I just about despise having to retrace my steps to find something I forgot or carelessly left in another part of the house after intending to bring it with me. With him coming through I went to get the thing without a second thought and without any reactivity, and that's a major shift regarding something that seems simple to anyone else but has been a struggle for me in life.

The reader had said that this life took place around 500 B.C.E. and that it was a Greek state that began with "S." I figured it was Sparta but looked up areas beginning with that letter that were active then. Sparta was the major military force on the planet at that time and the more I read about the city-state the more I felt at home, a recognition of who I on some level have thought I am. This other-life persona was making himself known for, really, the first time. When he was on the surface I recognized that I've always had him with me but that I have never known what to do with him or how to give him the time of day. I had always been working to unwind stress and become less wound up and reactive to just about everything. Even as I had often felt that a part of me could handle all of the little and big stressors life can present now and then in practice I was in fact not able to handle most things unless I was intentionally grounded and working extremely hard to focus on the present moment. Being filled with energy in your body – especially of a reactive warrior determined to make sure that nothing in the environment becomes a threat to you – leads away from a state of being able to respond on an even keel and being able to respond intentionally. Even my normal-to-date state of jumpiness – my startle response – lessened dramatically after this situation unfolded. For most of my life I had been on edge and almost everything startled me, seeing me jump in the air at little things in my environment.

I read about the hypermilitarization of Spartan society, particular battles and strategies employed for which the city-state was famous, weapons and shielding, the four castes that made up the society, the educational system that fed the elite class of Spartans, marriage customs, and other things. Every time in these texts there was a detail about plain dress or focused living, or the rationale behind training and life in this culture deeply focused on military life, this part of me felt more and more welcome to be on the surface. I told him that he is welcome to be here and that I'm ready to stand up for and defend myself in ways that my 8 year-old self could not. He indicated that to welcome and work with him I would need to get back in my body and treat it better and I decided I was willing to get back to that way of being. He specifically indicated that more and more consistent exercise is a key because – he indicated like a big brother or concerned teacher – when a man is in his body and knows what it can do, he can direct it toward the right tasks and condition it to be able to handle anything without flying off the handle.

One of the things I read about was the preparation of youth for lives as soldiers by working on their pain tolerance. I was able to connect with his memories and feelings about his rigorous training in the focused system called *agoge*. Some sense of violent treatment toward me in other lives that I have felt regularly I attributed to situations in which other mes on the timeline are being tortured for one reason or another. Since the other warrior left I've been able to detect that some of these memories are in fact from this Spartan's early life in training. He was able to keep them in context as he is a warrior but I have not. I have responded to the somewhat violent treatment he received from his peers and teachers without awareness of the context, in other words. To me it feels like torture and to him it is part of the education to become part of an elite fighting force. Having his level of awareness of some of these painful sense memories helps me make sense of them. This enables me also to make some peace with certain sense memories of violence and intentionally-inflicted pain that I carry now. I can separate a noticeable portion of them – with his help – from the sensation of outright torture that other experiences have on me.

As I read about cultural attitudes informed by the collective intention to devote much time and energy to developing a strong military, a number of things stood out as things about which we agree. In fact I am able to see that some of my basic attitudes stem from his training and lifestyle. Of all the stories in this book I relate more to his cultural context and intellectual and emotional response to them than any other. After I explained this story to J. she said that of all these parts this is the one she lives with on a day-to-day basis!

One example is the simple clothing and basic housing Spartans were to employ like all other Spartans. For years I wore primarily the same 4 gray t-shirts – they are identical, purchased at the same time – and when they began to show wear I went to purchase another set of 4. However when at the store I watched myself go through this through process I thought it silly – I was a bit embarrassed and not being open to any color. So I switched one for a green t-shirt, thinking I didn't need to be so rigid and plain. This was about two and a half years ago and I still feel odd about it! The situation is imbalanced.

Regarding housing, during my adult life I haven't sought to live in places I consider nice but have chosen rentals based on location or functionality. It got to the point that when J. moved in with me, we both saw starkly how minimalist I had become accustomed to live. The one-bedroom guest house was small at around 450 square feet but the furnishings were minimal. A bed, a small table with two chairs that were there when I moved in, a small dresser also there when I moved in, and boxes of my things were what filled the place. I remember I had a lamp, too, but not much else. In the kitchen I had a full set of dishes and a set of bowls in addition but I only ever used one of them at a time and a particular fork and knife. I owned other silverware but didn't see a need to use them.

This was fine for me because the guest house served as a writing studio and a place to do work with clients and students. When J. arrived to visit before moving to Arizona I found myself embarrassed as I tried to come up with an explanation for why everything was so spare and minimalist. She used the word "Spartan" in a non-judging way. With her my playful, Sagittarian side including my Moon is brought out directly and this way of living that I'd cultivated through nonvariation and choosing what seemed the most boring and pragmatic options suddenly seemed steps too far. My prominent Venus in Libra on the Libra Ascendant was entirely missing from my home! As my Venus began to emerge after a few years of not being in relationship, the contrast of how I had been living with how I am wired as a human was stark. As she moved in we had many conversations cut short wherein she would ask me if I owned this or that household object or tool and I would stare at her without answer. I could say I didn't have a dish rack, a vacuum (the floors were tile), or more than one lamp but it got to the point of embarrassment such that I didn't want to be asked anything else. I was starting to freeze up when it came to putting the house together because part of me could not see the point in investing time, energy, and money in creating a home. There was even a moment in a store after she moved in, where she had lead us to purchase household stuff and cleaning supplies. I froze in dissociation and somehow found the wherewithal to tell her that we should remember that a 4th-house NN can have one frozen in the headlights in the house wares aisle with the new girlfriend. To a large degree this was my 4th-house NN making itself seen – a lá a deer caught in the headlights – but I can see in retrospect the influence of this warrior who lives his life with single-minded focus and a willingness to sacrifice much in the way of how – his phrase – ordinary people live.

As I've discussed this other-life part and the role of his attitudes in my life, J. has reflected several times that among all the personas I've uncovered and discussed with her, this one is primary. She lives with a man who goes back and forth between loving, generous, kind, and sweet to utterly focused on his goals to the exclusion of everything else. She has become attuned to the switch and – thank the lords – does not take personally when she approaches me for a Venus moment and is met with this character from another part of the timeline who almost cannot see her beyond being someone who happens to be taking up space in the vicinity.

I've variously understood this motivation to achieve goals at almost any cost as a benefit as well as something to remain aware of and keep in check. In a 3-year period I wrote or channeled 12 books and I am clear that this Spartan's drive and focus were in constant play during that time. I was asked by a number of people along the way how I was producing so much work while continuing to develop my counseling astrology and channeling practice, being my own webmaster and marketer, and producing podcasts and courses. I told them that I was focused and motivated to move a lot of energy through words, that I had a goal and I knew how to make it happen and I put on hold things that didn't support achieving the goal. In part it is true that I had always identified as a writer but didn't have the self-confidence to do it or a topic I believed strongly enough needed to be explored through words and by me. But as soon as those two factors were in play I jumped in and didn't look back. Living a Spartan life enabled me to put words to all I was thinking as it bubbled up from under the surface during the transit of Pluto to my 3rd-house Jupiter in Capricorn. In the end it felt that I/my consciousness was a tube of toothpaste that Pluto had been progressively squeezing out and I was exhausted. But I am clear that this other-life warrior had been a major element in my motivation and work ethic during that time.

Regarding other details gained from my research after the Akashic Records reading, there are a number with which I found myself agreeing and to which I related as the Spartan inside me nodded his head with surety. The culturally-inspired logic makes sense to me on a deep level and yet I would not support the implementation of many in our society in modern times. One of these details was that male babies born in that society were evaluated at birth for deformities. Those with anything wrong with them and expected to be unable to grow into good warriors were left out in this particular place outside the city to die. The simplistic view that the cultural ideal of a strong military is all that matters echoes some black-and-white thinking I have had at times that holds that if there is a goal to be achieved, you must be willing to do anything to achieve it. In the minds of the Spartans the military strength they sought to and did create was worth everything to them. But I relate strongly to the notion that there must be sacrifices along the way in order to be the best at a given task or discipline.

Boys who survived went from their families at age 7 to be raised in cohorts in a military school setting, living and learning in small groups I read described as herds. In retrospect I can see one thread of my feelings toward family is that I sometimes feel that I shouldn't have to bother with them (ouch - that is hard to admit!). Other parts of me find this embarrassing and I have not talked about it with anyone. Reading about the lifestyle of dedication to their messes (the name for the cohorts they grew up, lived, trained, and fought with from ages 7 to 30) made much sense to me in terms of the feeling I have that I was for many years looking for something to which to dedicate myself and family always seemed in the way. At various times I've understood this in terms of the vocabulary associated with my nodal structure, with the NN in the 4th house, that of home, family, heritage, and community – a thing that's been left out of my karmic history and therefore my preferences and comfort zones is family and belonging. This Spartan's 10th house community is intended to serve all the functions of his 4th house. What I can see now is that being surrounded by colleagues who are trained in and as dedicated to the same ideals that you are eliminates the messiness that can come with having commitments to family members instead. At age 20 they were permitted to marry but they would not live with their spouses and children until age 30. At times I've had the sense that for the time being I am focusing on my work and there is no need to rush to think about having a family. Perhaps this other-life persona within me is waiting until I'm 30 to begin thinking about the topic, not grasping that fact that I am already 40! When I'm asked if I want to have children my first reaction is to know with certainty that I don't have to have an answer. This seems to me at least in part related to the life of this man on the other part of the timeline, so focused on and dedicated to his single chosen mission in life.

Age 30 is when they were considered ready to enter into society with full rights and privileges. At that age they could hold public office and vote. The other three castes and all the younger Spartans-in-training were not involved in these processes, leading to an obvious oligarchy leaving out the majority of the population. From my research and the feeling of his I carry within me – that now I can discern is one subpersona and not really about who Tom Jacobs is – the entirety of his training to be a Spartan had built into it a sense that they were the elite not just in their own world but on the entire planet. My research reflects that as a military power they were respected and feared (or respected because of the fear?) above all else. This man as he has come through me during this life has carried this sense and I have been worried about being found out to be a raging snob! This part of me expects to be treated well and with the respect that I've deserved from my accomplishments (if I've been doing well) and when I notice that I live a relatively ordinary life this part of me find this confusing. I have noted that most of my adult jobs have been with companies that are doing cutting-edge research or work and this part of me takes pride in this.

The standards of conduct and expectations of Spartans were high and punishment for doing something out of line were severe. If a Spartan did something considered beneath him or his station as elite it was easy to be demoted to the status of free citizen, one having none of the rights and privileges reserved for Spartans. Once this happened he could never hope to be elevated again and neither could any of his descendants. Under the surface this part of me has held what I can only call severe opinions about respectability. This is one of those areas in which I carry an opinion upon which I don't act much but I have held myself to a high standard in all that I do and found it difficult when I don't measure up for whatever reason.

Another detail about the standards of this other-life way of being including not consuming alcohol. This is one of the activities avoided because, he says, the effects get in the way of being the best one can be at all times. From what I gather it might have been considered a mark of sloppiness and not being in control of one's life or disciplined. To teach young Spartans-to-be a lesson it is said that members of the serf caste would be forced alcohol to excess and then brought in to them and displayed as drunken train-wreck object lessons about the dangers of losing self-control. The point for me is that I have at times had a strong opinion about alcohol and especially about those people who drink too much at any given time or often. I have compassion for the kinds of situations and emotional dynamics that can lead to that lifestyle but this Spartan within me wants nothing to do with anyone drinking too much. My feeling is that there is nothing wrong with alcohol and I do consume it some. Since my intuitive opening at age 30 I've consumed a lot less alcohol primarily because since that time I regularly have felt that I'm under the influence of substances and experience altered states of consciousness without doing or consuming anything. I enjoy it some now and this part of me has definite opinions about how much is too much both in me and others.

There's a difference between the military officer described in an earlier chapter. The Prussian officer you met in an earlier chapter enjoys life and physical pleasures including alcohol. He's the kind of guy you'd find making a lot of joyful noise with others at a local pub. He does his job well and takes it seriously but not nearly as seriously as the Spartan. With the latter there is a single-minded focus on a goal and there is little room for deviation but also no motivation to deviate – achieving the goal will be great so why waste a lot of time along the way?

I see this other life as related to Pluto in the 12th house because one of the ways that surrender can be experienced is to an ideal. In this man's case it was to the mythology and social cohesion built around constructing the perfect military. This ideal might not appeal to many now but we do not live in the cultural context that he does. His entire society is built around an ideal. Another side of the 12th house is to go big, to seem or attempt to manifest in the material world something universal. Submitting to the ideals of a hypermilitarized society can involve seeing warriors as bigger than life, a very 12th-house image.

Regarding Mars-Uranus in the 1st house square the nodal axis, I think the connection should be obvious. There is Mars work to be done in finding the right way (square the nodes) to assert the self and take action. As a child I came in with some fear about expressing my Mars energy and so at times it rushed in to find me – the vacuum effect – as outlined elsewhere in this volume. Then in a moment of trauma the other-life contract became due and I was filled with the consciousness of this karma mate who was primed to help me defend my 8 year-old self. The result was that I was filled with his angry warrior energy and unable to find a middle ground. Connecting Uranus here, many Mars experiences for manifestations of my soul across the Earth timeline will experience them as sudden, original, or traumatic. This episode with the nurse at age 8 in this life fits as does the Spartan's experiences being an elite warrior. Uranus can indicate being ahead of the curve as well as being in possession of an ability to detach from emotions and other elements of self in order to remain objective enough to achieve a goal. At this stage in my life as Tom Jacobs I understand a great deal about how *not* to do Mars-Uranus! If I'm too quiet then I draw sudden, fiery experiences to show me that this energy is within me – that I need to own it and express it. If I act out that energy without thinking then I run the risk of traumatizing myself. This other-life Spartan has for the several last weeks been helping me see how to carry myself – both my energy field (related to attitude and intention) and my physical body – to embody the right sort of Mars-Uranus energy. I can tell that he doesn't think about this way of being but has been conditioned to live it. Energies in the 1st house we can't spend too much time thinking about. We need to live them in unselfconscious ways if we are to do them justice because they are elements of our personalities that we feel instinctively. Thinking can take us out of the moment when it comes to 1st-house placements and we just need to flow with them to let them do what they need to do.

Afterword

Yesterday, after nearly finishing a first draft of this volume, I found myself utterly freaked out during a preview at a movie theater. J. and I went to see a snazzy little picture in 3D on the super cool screen with the awesome audio set up. With the 3D glasses on I saw the spears thrown from the natives at the invaders coming at my face and I clenched up with fear. Hand flew to cover eyes and I squeezed the expletives out of J.'s hand. At first I thought it related to the other-life part in the second-to-last chapter (A Woman Who Lost Her Mind) but a few minutes later I saw that there's contact and integration waiting for me with different lives in which my soul's manifestations experience violence through war and other contexts. Making contact with the Spartan described in the last chapter is a great first step but there are others. I've had issues with drawing violence and accidents to me in this life and have not yet been able to fully deal with those pasts. What I've been able to do is decide that I am safe and cease drawing those kinds of situations to me in this life, and this certainly is progress. Yet I know there is more to do.

What I consider emotional evidence about this includes the deep response to the song "Over There" mentioned early on in the book. Also there is a series of experiences I had during Hellinger Constellation Groups in which I was chosen to represent a series of young men who went off to war and never came back. Then there is the sense that what is useful about me would be wasted on being drafted and going to war, an argument I had with an all-American type youth in a high school US History class. He felt I was unpatriotic and I felt like I'd been there and done it and would be better used in some sort of thinking capacity. I think it was a sort of defense strategy to avoid the thought of being in battle.

Oh, and then there were all the years when neighbors set off fireworks in the street or their yards at the 4th of July and New Year's, when I would sit in my house and try to keep out the terror that I was under attack and that everything was wrong and would be lost. Long before beginning intuitive work and learning some of the processes described in this book it looked like being seized with terror and not understanding why. After years of hating these holidays with a passion[19] I realized they were not bombs and started to make progress dealing with it and eventually getting over it. At a park watching fireworks, outside and with others in a festive mood, but things exploding when I'm indoors and can't see them was a problem.

---

[19] As well as the people who were setting the fireworks off, for whom I reserved the term "yahoos."

All of this is to say that even with all the stories in this book lived and processed, there are more under the surface to work with. I know that both sides of violence, killing, war, and death across time are waiting for me to deal with. I wonder if integrating the other-life woman who felt she had lost her mind might open a door to that. Even when it was happening I was clear that being able to stay grounded while replaying the horrific image from the documentary in order to calm the part down was a turning point in working with intense emotions and memories.

So we'll see what's next. I can't say that I won't sometimes wish I am not reliving whatever rises to the surface but I know I'll be able to work with it.

About the Author

The photo J. took on the hike in LA referenced in "A Man Who Loses Everything."

Tom Jacobs is an Evolutionary Astrologer and Channel. A graduate of Evolutionary Astrologer Steven Forrest's Apprenticeship Program, Tom has a global practice of readings, coaching, tutoring, and energy work to help people understand what they came to Earth to do and supporting them in making it happen. He is the author and channel of books on astrology, mythology, and spirituality as well as original astrological natal reports on Lilith and emotional healing. Contact Tom Jacobs via http://tdjacobs.com.

26175284R00143

Made in the USA
Lexington, KY
22 September 2013